Lewis Morris

Songs of Two Worlds,

Third Series

Lewis Morris

Songs of Two Worlds,
Third Series

ISBN/EAN: 9783744777643

Printed in Europe, USA, Canada, Australia, Japan

Cover: Foto ©Thomas Meinert / pixelio.de

More available books at **www.hansebooks.com**

SONGS OF TWO WORLDS

(THIRD SERIES)

BY

A NEW WRITER

Μηδὲν ἄγαν.

SECOND EDITION

HENRY S. KING & CO.
65 CORNHILL, AND 12 PATERNOSTER ROW, LONDON
1876

(All rights reserved.)

PREFACE.

THE writer fulfils in the present volume the promise made in the last,—of a third and concluding series of "Songs of Two Worlds."

The result of his former attempts hardly leaves him, as he could wish, at liberty to bring his contributions to English verse to a definite close. But to become a voluminous verse-writer is so far from his desire, that the chance of his writing no more is at least sufficiently great to warrant him in bidding his many unknown friends a cordial, though perhaps not a final, farewell.

PREFACE TO THE SECOND EDITION.

THE writer's warmest acknowledgements are due to the whole of the critical press and to the public for their generous appreciation of his verse, and for the very flattering expression of their wish that the present volume may not be his last.

If he should not again challenge their favourable verdict, it will be from any cause rather than ingratitude; but, in any case, he feels it best that "Songs of Two Worlds" should now come to an end.

CONTENTS.

	PAGE
Song	1
The Home Altar	3
The Voyage	5
The Food of Song	7
The Youth of Thought	10
Song	17
At Chambers	18
Evensong	21
Song	66
At Last	68
A Memorial	72
Song	78
The Dialogue	80
The Birth of Verse	82
From Hades	84
Song	105

Contents.

	PAGE
The Enigma	100
To the Tormentors	112
Children of the Street	117
Song	127
A Separation Deed	128
An Ode to Free Rome ...	131
The Wreck	155
Wasted	156
Sursum!	157
Song	159
Anchored	160
Souls in Prison	163
Frederic	168
To my Motherland	171

———o———

SONGS OF TWO WORLDS.

(THIRD SERIES.)

SONG.

Tell me where I may quench the too fierce fire
Of hope and of desire;
Tell me how I may from my soul remove
The sting and pain of love;
Tell me, and I will give to thee,
Magician, my whole soul in fee.

And yet I know not what of fit reward,
For enterprise so hard,
I might convey thee in a loveless soul,
Whose currents no more roll:
A corpse, corruptible and cold,
Were no great prize to have and hold.

Time only is it that will deign to take
Such things for their own sake,
Preferring age to youth, grey hairs to brown,
And to bright smiles the frown.
Time takes the hope, Time dulls the smart,
And first makes slow, then stops the heart.

Wherefore to Time I will address my song.
Time, equable and strong,
Take thou all hopes and longings clean away—
And yet I prithee stay :
Forbear, for rather I would be
Consumed, than turn to ice with thee.

———o———

THE HOME ALTAR.

Why should we seek at all to gain
By vigils, and in pain,
By lonely life and empty heart,
To set a soul apart
Within a cloistered cell,
For whom the precious, homely hearth would serve as well?

There, with the early breaking morn,
Ere quite the day is born,
The lustral waters flow serene,
And each again grows clean;
From sleep, as from a tomb,
Born to another day of joy, and hope, and doom.

There through the sweet and toilsome day,
To labour is to pray;
There love with kindly beaming eyes
Prepares the sacrifice;
And voice and innocent smile
Of childhood do our cheerful liturgies beguile.

There, at his chaste and frugal feast,
Love sitteth as a Priest;
And with mild eyes and mien sedate,
His deacons stand and wait;
And round the holy table
Paten and chalice range in order serviceable.

And when ere night, the vespers said,
Low lies each weary head,
What giveth He who gives them sleep,
But a brief death less deep?
Or what the fair dreams given
Than ours who, daily dying, dream a happier heaven?

Then not within a cloistered wall
Will we expend our days;
But dawns that break and eves that fall
Shall bring their dues of praise.
This best befits a Ruler always near,
This duteous worship mild, and reasonable fear.

———o———

THE VOYAGE.

Who climbs the Equatorial main
Drives on long time through mist and cloud,
Through zones of storm, through thunders loud,
For many a night of fear and pain.

Till one night all is clear, and lo!
He sees with wondering, awe-struck eyes,
In depths above, in depths below,
Strange constellations light the skies—

New stars, more splendid and more fair,
Yet not without a secret loss :
He seeks in vain the Northern Bear,
And finds instead the Southern Cross.

Yet dawns the self-same sun—the same
The deep below the keel which lies ;
Though this may burn with brighter flame,
And that respond to bluer skies,

The self-same earth, the self-same sky:
And though through clouds and tempests driven,
The self-same seeker lifts an eye
That sees another side of heaven.

No change in man, or earth, or aught,
Save those strange secrets of the night;
Nor there, save that another thought
Has reached them through another sight,

Which may but know one hemisphere,
The earth's mass blotting out the blue,
Till one day, leaving shadows here,
It sees all heaven before its view.

———o———

THE FOOD OF SONG.

How best doth vision come
To the poet's mind,—
Lonely beneath the blue, unclouded dome,
Or battling with the mighty ocean-wind;
In fair spring mornings, with the soaring lark,
Or amid roaring midnight forests dark?

Shall he attune his voice
To sweetest song,
When earth and sea and sky alike rejoice,
And men are blest, and think no thought of wrong,
In some ideal heaven, some happy isle,
Where life is stiffened to a changeless smile?

Or best amid the noise
Of high designs,
Loud onsets, shatterings, awful battle joys,
Wherefor the loftier spirit longs and pines;
Or amid seething depths of leaden sea;
Or to loud thunders rolling dreadfully?

Nature is less than nought
In smile or frown,
But for the formless, underlying thought
Of mind and purpose greater than our own ;
This only can these empty shows inform,
Smiles through the calm, and animates the storm.

Nor yet the clang and rush
Of mightier thought,
The steeps, the snows, the gulfs, that whelm and crush
The seeker with the treasure he has sought ;
Too vast, too swift, too formless to inspire
The fictive hand, or touch the lips with fire.

But rather mid the throng
Of toiling men
He finds the food and sustenance of song,
Spread by hidden hands, again, and yet again,
Where'er he goes, by crowded city street,
He fares thro' springing fancies sad and sweet—

Some innocent baby smile ;
A close-wound waist ;
Fathers and children ; things of shame and guile ;
Dim eyes, and lips at parting kissed in haste ;

The halt, the blind, the prosperous thing of ill;
The thief, the wanton, touch and vex him still.

Or if sometimes he turn
With a new thrill,
And strives to paint anew with words that burn
The inner thought of sea, or sky, or hill:
It is because a breath of human life
Has touched them: joy and suffering, rest and strife.

And he sees mysteries
Above, around,
Fair spiritual fleeting agencies
Haunting each foot of consecrated ground.
And so, these fading, raises bolder eyes
Beyond the furthest limits of the skies,

And every thought and word,
And all things seen,
And every passion which his heart has stirred,
And every joy and sorrow which has been,
And every step of life his feet have trod,
Lead by broad stairs of glory up to God.

———o———

THE YOUTH OF THOUGHT.

Oh happy days ! oh joyous time !
    When thought was gay and man was young,
And to a golden flow of rhyme,
    Life like a melody was sung;

When, in the springtime of the earth,
    The cloud-capt hill, the dewy grove,
Clear lake and rippling stream gave birth
    To shy Divinities of love;

When often to the jovial feast
    Of love or wine the people came,
And Nature was the only priest
    And Youth and Pleasure knew not shame.

Nor darker shape of wrong or ill
    The fearful fancy might inspire,
Than vine-crowned on some shady hill,
    The Satyr nursing quaint desire.

The Youth of Thought.

And if some blooming youth or maid
   In depths of wood or stream were lost,
Some love-lorn Deity, 'twas said,
   The blissful truant's path had crossed.

Sweet time of fancy, giving place
   To times of thinking scarce less blest,
When Wisdom wore a smiling face,
   And Knowledge was like Fancy drest,

And Art with Language lived ingrown,
   The cunning hand and golden tongue;
By this the form Divine was shown,
   By that its deathless praises sung.

When in cool temples fair and white,
   By purple sea, or myrtle shade,
The gods took shape to mortal sight,
   By their own creatures' hands re-made.

And daily, mid the cheerful noise
   Of wrestling, or the panting race—
Through the clear laughter of the boys,
   And tender forms of youthful grace—

Grave sages walked in high debate
    Beneath the laurel grove, and sought
To solve the mysteries of Fate,
    And sound the lowest deeps of Thought;

Nor knew that they, as those indeed,
    Were naked, taking fair for right;
With beauty only for all creed,
    Yet not without some heaven-sent light.

Now preaching clear the deathless soul;
    Now winging love from sloughs of shame;
And oft from earthly vapours foul,
    Soaring aloft with tongues of flame.

Knew they no inward voice to vex
    The careless joyance of their way—
No pointing finger stern, which checks
    The sad transgressor of to-day?

Fair dream, if any dream be fair,
    Which knows no fuller life than thine;
Which only moves through earthly air,
    And builds on shadows half divine;

The Youth of Thought.

How art thou fled! For us no more
    Dryad or Satyr haunts the grove;
No Nereid sports upon the shore,
    Nor with wreathed horn the Tritons rove;

Who breathe a fuller, graver air,
    Long since to manhood's stature grown;
Who leave our childhood's fancies fair,
    For pains and pleasures of our own.

For us no more the young vine climbs,
    Its gadding tendrils flinging down;
Who move in sadder, wiser times,
    Whose thorns are woven for a crown.

The lily and the passion-flower
    Preach a new tale of gain and loss,
And in the wood-nymph's closest bower
    The springing branches form the cross.

"A great hope traversing the earth,"
    Has taken all the young world's bloom,
And for the joy and flush of birth,
    Has left the solemn thought of doom;

And made the body no more divine,
　　And built our Heaven no longer here;
And given for joyous fancies fine,
　　Souls bowed with holy awe and fear.

And far beyond the suns, removed
　　The godhead seen by younger eyes,
Far from the people once beloved,
　　And girt by dreadful mysteries.

Fulfilled with thoughts, more fair and dear
　　Than all the lighter joys of yore,
Immeasurable hopes brought near,
　　And Heaven laid open more and more.

But not with love and peace alone
　　Time came, which older joys could take;
But with fierce brand and hopeless groan,
　　Red war, the dungeon, and the stake;

And lives by Heaven too much opprest,
　　And cloisters dim with tears and sighs,
And young hearts withered in the breast,
　　And fasts and stripes and agonies.

And for Apollo breathing strength,
    And Aphrodité warm with life ;
A tortured Martyr come at length,
    To the last pang of lifelong strife.

While round us daily move no more
    Those perfect forms of youthful grace,
No more men worship as before
    The rounded limb, the clear-cut face.

Who see the dwarfed mechanic creep,
    With hollow cheek, and lungs that bleed,
Or the swart savage fathoms deep,
    Who comes to air, to sleep, and breed.

Aye, but by loom, or forge, or mine,
    Or squalid hut, there breaks for these
Hope more immense, awe more divine
    Than ever dawned on Sokrates.

While if we seek to live again
    In careless lives the pagan charm,
We only prove a life long pain,
    For that clear conscience void of harm.

For in the manhood of God's days
    We live, and not in careless youth;
The essence more than form we praise,
    And Beauty moves us less than Truth.

From youth to age; till cycles hence
    Another and a higher spring,
And with a truer innocence,
    Again the world shall think and sing.

———o———

SONG.

I WOULD thou might'st not vex me with thine eyes,
   Thou fair Ideal Beauty, nor would'st shame
All lower thoughts and visions as they rise,
   As in mid-noon a flame.

For now thy presence leaves no prospect fair,
   Nor joy in act, nor charm in any maid,
Nor end to be desired, for which men dare,
   Thou making me afraid.

Because life seems through thee a thing too great
   To spend on these, which else might grow to thee;
So that fast bound, I idly hesitate:
   I prithee set me free;

Or, hold me, if thou wilt, but come not near,
   Let me pursue thee still in ghostly grace;
Far off let me pursue thee, for I fear
   To faint before thy face.

———o———

AT CHAMBERS.

To the chamber, where now uncaring
    I sit apart from the strife,
While the fool and the knave are sharing
    The pleasures and profits of life,

There came a faint knock at the door,
    Not long since on a terrible day;
One faint little knock, and no more;
    And I brushed the loose papers away.

And as no one made answer, I rose,
    With quick step and impatience of look,
And a glance of the eye which froze,
    And a ready voice of rebuke.

But when the door opened, behold!
    A mother, low-voiced and mild,
Whose thin shawl and weak arms enfold
    A pale little two-year-old child.

What brought her there? Would I relieve her?
    Was all the poor mother could say;
For her child, scarce recovered from fever,
    Left the hospital only that day.

Pale, indeed, was the child; yet so cheerful,
    That, seeing me wonder, she said,
Of doubt and repulse, grown fearful,
    " Please look at his dear little head;"

And snatched off the little bonnet,
    And so in a moment laid bare
A shorn little head, and upon it
    No trace of the newly-come hair.

When, seeing the stranger's eye
    Grow soft, with an innocent guile
The child looked up, shrinking and shy,
    With the ghost of a baby smile.

Poor child! I thought, so soon come
    To the knowledge of lives oppressed,
To whom poverty comes with home,
    And sickness brings food and rest:

Who art launched forth, a frail little boat,
    In the midst of life's turbulent sea,
To be sunk, it may be, or to float
    On great waves that care nothing for thee.

What awaits thee? An early peace
    In the depth of a little grave,
Or, despite all thy ills to increase,
    Through some dark chance, mighty to save;

Till in stalwart manhood you meet
    The strong man, who regards you to-day,
Crawling slowly along the street,
    In old age withered and gray?

Who knows? But the thoughts I have told
    In one instant flashed through my brain,
As the poor mother, careful of cold,
    Clasped her infant to her again.

And I, if I searched for my purse,
    Was I selfish, say you, and wrong?
Surely silver is wasted worse
    Than in earning the right to a song.

EVENSONG.

The hymns and the prayers were done, and the village
    church was still,
As I lay in a waking dream in the churchyard upon the
    hill.

The graves were all around, and the dark yews over my
    head,
And below me the winding stream and the exquisite
    valley were spread.

The sun was sloping down with a glory of dying rays,
And the hills were bathed in gold, and the woods were
    vocal with praise.

But from the deep set valley there rose a vapour of grey,
And the sweet day sank, and the glory waxed fainter and
    faded away.

Then there came, like a chilling wind, a cold, low
    whisper of doubt,
Which silenced the echo of hymns, and blotted the
    glories out.

And I wrestled with powers unseen, and strove with a Teacher divine,
Like Jacob who strove with the angel, and found with the dawn a sign.

*   *   *   *

For I thought of the words they sing: It is He that hath made us indeed;
And my thought flew back to the fathers of thought and their atheist creed—

How atom with atom at first fortuitously combined,
Formed all, from the worlds without to the innermost worlds of mind;

And I thought: What, if this be true, and no Maker there is indeed,
And God is the symbol alone of a feeble and worn-out creed;

And from uncreate atoms, impelled by a blind chance driving on free,
Grew together the primal forms of all essences that be!

Then a voice: If they were, indeed, they were separate one from one
By a gulph as broad as yawns in space betwixt sun and sun—

Self-centred and self-contained, disenvironed and isolate;
Drawn together by a hidden love, torn apart by a hidden hate.

What power was this—chance, will you say? But chance, what else can it mean
Than the hidden Cause of things by human reason unseen?

Chance! Then Chance were a name for God, or each atom bearing a soul
Indivisible, like with like, part and whole of the Infinite Whole.

Were God, as the Pantheist taught, God in earth, and in sky, and in air,
God through every thought and thing, and made manifest everywhere;

The spring and movement of things—the stir, the breathing of breath,
Without which all things were quenched in the calm of an infinite death;

Or, if within each there lay some germ of an unborn power,
God planted it first, God quickened, God raised it from seed to flower.

Though beneath the weird cosmical force, which we wield and yet cannot name,
From the germ or the rock we draw out low gleams of life's faintest flame;

Though we lose the will that commands, and the muscles that wait and serve,
In some haze of a self-set spring of the molecules of nerve;

Though we sink all spirit in matter, and let the Theogonies die,
Life and death are; thinker and thought; outward, inward; I, and not I;

And the I is the Giver of life, and without it the matter
    must die.

  * * * * *

Then I ceased for a while from thought, as I lay on the
    long green grass,
Hearing echoes of hymns anew, and letting the moments
    pass.

The evening was mounting upward; the sunbeams had
    left the hill;
But the dying daylight lingered, and all the valley was
    still.

  * * * * *

Then I said: But if God there be, how shall man by his
    thinking find,
Who is only a finite creature, the depths of the Infinite
    Mind—

Who sounds with a tiny plummet, who scans with a
    purblind eye,
The depths of that fathomless ocean, the wastes of that
    limitless sky?

Shall we bow to a fetish, a symbol, which maybe neither
    sees nor hears;
Or, seeing and hearing indeed, takes no thought for our
    hopes or fears;

Who is dumb, though we long for a word; who is deaf,
    though his children cry;
Who is Master, yet bears with evil—Lord, and lets all
    precious things die?

Or if in despair we turn from the godless and meaningless
    plan,
What do we, but make for ourselves a God in the image
    of man—

A creature of love and hate, a creature who makes for
    good,
But barred by an evil master from working the things
    that he would?

If he be not a reflex image, we may not know him at all;
If he be, we are God ourselves—to ourselves we shall
    stand or fall.

Then the voice : But what folly is this ! Cannot God
    indeed be known,
If we know not the hidden essence that forms Him and
    builds his throne?

Is all our knowledge nought, of sea, and of sky, and of
    star,
Till we know them, not as they seem to our thinking, but
    as they are?

We who build the whole fabric of knowledge on vague
    abstractions sublime;
We who whirl through an infinite space, and live in an
    infinite time;

We who prate of Motion and Force, not knowing that
    on either side
Black gulphs unavoidable yawn, dark riddles our thought
    deride ;

Shall we hold our science as nought of all things of
    earth, because
We know but the seemings and shows, the relations, and
    not the cause—

Not only as he who admires the rainbow and cloud of gold,
Knows that 'tis but a form of vapour his wondering eyes behold;

But as he who sees and knows, and knowing would fain ignore
What he knows since the essence of things is hid, and he knows not more—

Or who would not love his love, or walk hand in hand with his friend,
Since he sees not the roots of the tree from whose branches life's blossoms depend?

Or how should the sight we see, any more than the sound we hear,
Be a thing which exists for our thought, apart from the eye or the ear;

Is not every atom of dust, which compacted we call the earth,
A miracle baffling our thought with insoluble wonders of birth?

And know we not, indeed, that the matter which men have taught,
Is itself an essence unseen and untouched—but by spirit and thought?

Tush! It is but a brainsick dream. What was it that taught us the laws
Which stand as a bar between us and the thought of the Infinite Cause?

Is he infinite, out of relation, and absolute, past finding out?
Reach we not an antinomy here? feel we here no striving of doubt?

How, then, shall the finite define the bounds of the infinite plan,
This is finite, and infinite this: here is Deity, here is man.

If our judgment be relative only, how then shall our brain transcend
The limits of relative thought grown too eager to comprehend?

For he passes the bounds of relation, if any there be who can
Distinguish the absolute God from the relative in man :

He has bridged the gulph; he has leaped o'er the bound; he has seen with his eyes
For a moment the land unseen, that beyond the mountain peaks lies.

Nay! we see but a part of God, since we gaze with a finite sight;
And yet not Darkness is He, but a blinding splendour of light.

Do we shrink from this light, and let our dazzled eyeballs fall?
Nay! a God fully known or utterly dark, were not God at all.

Though we hold not that in some sphere which our thought may never conceive,
There comes not a time when to know may be all, and not to believe;

Nor yet that the right which we love, and the wrong which we hate to-day,
May not show as reversed, or as one, when the finite has passed away;

God we know in our image indeed, since we are in the image of Him,
Of His splendour a faint low gleam, of His glory a reflex dim.

Bowing not to the all unknown, nor to that which is searched out quite;
But to That which is known, yet unknown—to the darkness that comes of light,
To the contact of God with man, to the struggle and triumph of right.

*　*　*　*　*

Then I ceased for a while from thought, as I lay on the long green grass,
Hearing echoes of hymns grown nearer, and letting the moments pass.

Exult, oh dust and ashes! the low voices seemed to say;
And then came a sudden hush, and the jubilance faded away.

The evening was dying now, and the moon-rise was on the hill,
And the soft light touched the river, and all the valley was still.

* * * * *

Then I thought: But if God there be, and our thought may reach Him indeed,
How should this bare knowledge alone stand in lieu of a fuller creed?

If He be and is good, as they say, how yet can our judgment approve,
'Mid the rule of His iron laws, the place of His infinite love?

The rocks are built up of death, earth and sea teem with ravin and wrong;
The sole law in Nature we learn, is the law that strengthens the strong.

Through countless ages of time, the Lord has withdrawn Him apart
From all the world He has made, save the world of the human heart.

Without and within all is pain, from the cry of the child at birth,
To its parting sigh in age, when it looks for a happier earth.

Should you plead that God's order goes forth with a measured footstep sublime,
Know you not that you thrust Him back thus to the first beginnings of time,—

That a spark, a moment, a flash, and His work was over and done;
And the worlds were sent forth for ever, each circling around its sun.

Bearing with it all secrets of being, all potencies undefined,
All forms and changes of matter, all growths and achievements of mind.

What is there for our worship in this, and should not our reason say,
He is, and made us indeed, but hides Him too far away?

Though He lives, yet is He as one dead; and we, who would prostrate fall
Before the light of His Presence, we see not nor know Him at all.

Then the voice: Oh folly of doubt! what is time that we deem so far,
What else but a multiple vast of the little lives that are?

He who lives for the fifty years, which scarce rear thought to its prime,
Already a measure has lived of a thousand years of time.

Twice this, and Christ spoke not yet, and from this what a span appears,
The space till our thought is lost in the mists of a million years!

A thousand millions of years—we have leapt with a thought, with a word;
To the time when no flutter of life 'neath the shield of the trilobite stirred.

All time is too brief for our thought, and yet we would
 bring God nigh,
Till He worked in His creature's sight, man standing
 undazzled by.

Such a God were not God indeed ; nor, if He should
 change at all,
Should we hold, as we hold Him now, the God of both
 great and small.

How know we the great things from small ? how mark we
 the adequate cause,
Which might make the Creator impede the march of His
 perfect laws,—

We, who know but a part, not the whole ? Or were it a
 fitting thought
He should stoop in our sight to amend the errors His
 hand had wrought,

So His laws were not perfect at all ? or should he amend
 them indeed,
How supply by a fitful caprice the want of a normal
 creed ?

All life is a mode of force, and all force that is force must move;
'Tis a friction of Outward and Inward, a contrast of Hatred and Love.

Joy and Grief, Right and Wrong, Life and Death, Finite, Infinite, Matter and Will,
These are the twin wheels of the Chariot of Life, which without them stood still.

Would you seek in an order reversed and amended a Hand divine?
Nay, the Wonder of wonders lies in unchangeable design.

Should God break His law as He might; should He stoop from His infinite skies
To redress that which seems to us wrong, to raise up the life that dies;

Should He save from His wolf His lamb, from His tiger His innocent child;
Should He quench the fierce flames as they burn, or the great waves clamouring wild,

I think a great cry would go up from an orderless Universe,
And all the fair fabric of things would wither, as under a curse.

'Tis the God of the savage, is this. What do we who rise by degrees
To the gift of the mind that perceives, and the gift of the eye that sees?

Do not all our natures tend to a law of unbending rule,
Till equity comes but to mend the law that was made by the fool?

Who shows highest?—the child or the savage, whose smiles change to rage or to tears?
Or the statesman moving, unmoved, through a nation's desires and fears?

Or the pilgrim whose eyes look onward, as if to a distant home,
Never turning aside from his path, whatever allurements may come?

All Higher is more Unmoved; and the more unbroken
    the law,
The more sure does the Giver show to the eyes of a
    wondering awe.

Nor is it with all of truth that they make their voices
    complain,
Who weary our thought with tales of a constant ruin and
    pain.

It is but a brain-sick dream that would gloat o'er the
    hopeless bed,
Or the wreck, or the crash, or the fight, with their tales of
    the dying and dead.

Pain comes; hopeless pain, God knows and we know,
    again and again;
But even pain has its intervals blest, when 'tis heaven to
    be free from pain.

And I think that the wretch who lies pressed by a load of
    incurable ill,
With a grave pity pities himself, but would choose to have
    lived to it still;

And, as he whom the tiger bears in his jaws to his blood-
 stained den
Feels no pain nor fear, but a wonder what comes in the
 wonderful " Then,"

He pities himself and yet knows, as he casts up life's
 chequered sum,
It were best on the whole to have lived, whatever calamity
 come.

And the earth is full of joy. Every blade of grass that
 springs;
Every cool worm that crawls content as the eagle on
 soaring wings;

Every summer day instinct with life; every dawn when
 from waking bird
And morning hum of the bee, a chorus of praise is
 heard;

Every gnat that sports in the sun for his little life of a
 day;
Every flower that opens its cup to the dews of a perfumed May;

Every child that wakes with a smile, and sings to the
    ceiling at dawn ;
Every bosom which knows a new hope stir beneath its
    virginal lawn ;

Every young soul, ardent and high, rushing forth into life's
    hot fight ;
Every home of happy content, lit by love's own mystical
    light ;

Every worker who works till the evening, and takes before
    night his wage,
Be his work a furrow straight-drawn, or the joy of a
    bettered age ;

Every thinker who, standing aloof from the throng, finds
    a high delight
In striking with voice or with pen a stroke for the
    triumph of right ;—

All these know that life is sweet; all these, with a
    consonant voice,
Read the legend of Time with a smile, and that which
    they read is, " Rejoice ! "

    *   *   *   *   *

Then again I ceased from thought, as I lay on the long green grass,
Hearing hymns which grew fuller and fuller, and letting the moments pass.

Exult, oh dust and ashes! exult and rejoice! they said,
For blessed are they who live, and blessed are they who are dead.

Then again they ceased and were still, and my thought began once more,
But touched with a silvery gleam of hopes that were hidden before.

The moon had climbed up in the sky, far above the pines on the hill,
And the river ran molten silver, and all the valley was still.

* * * * *

Then I said: But if God there be, who made us indeed and is good,
What guide has He left for our feet to walk in the ways that He would?

For though He should speak indeed, yet, as soon as His voice grew dumb,
It were only through human speech that the message it bore might come,

Sunk to levels of human thought, and always marred and confined
By the chain of a halting tongue, and the curse of a finite mind;

So that he who would learn, indeed, what precepts His will has taught,
Must dim with a secular learning the brightness his soul has sought.

Who can tell how those scattered leaves through gradual ages grew,
Adding chaff and dust from the world to the accents simple and true?

If one might from the seer's wild visions, or stories of fraud and blood,
Or lore of the world-worn Sultan, discern the sure voice of good,

Such a mind were a God to itself; or if you should answer, For each
God has set a sure mentor within, with power to convince and teach;

Yet it speaks with a changeful voice, which alters with race and clime,
Nay, even in the self-same lands is changed with the changes of time;

So that 'twixt the old Europe of story and that which we know to-day,
Yawns a gulph, as wide almost as parts us from far Cathay;

What power has such voice to help us? Or if we should turn instead
To the precious dissonant pages, which keep what the Teacher said;

How reduce them to one indeed, or how seek in vain to ignore
The forgotten teachers who taught His counsels of mercy before?

Not "an eye for an eye" alone, was the rule which they loved to teach,
But Mercy, and Pity, and Love, though they spoke with a halting speech,

And He spake with the tongue of those who had spoken and then were dumb,
And clothed in the words of the Law, which He loved, would his precepts come ;

Nor always perfect was He in thought, in act, or in word,
Who withered in haste the fig-tree, and drove to destruction the herd ;

Who was angry sometimes, and spoke with quick words and fiery hate ;
Who offered too-perfect counsels, and took little thought for the State.

Other teachers have drawn more millions, who follow more faithful than we ;
Other teachers have taught a rule as stern and unselfish as He.

If we shrink from the Caliph fierce, who carved out a faith with his sword,
What say we of the pilgrim who sways the old East with his gentle word?

Or what of the sage whose vague words, over populous wastes of earth,
Have led millions of fettered feet to the grave from the day of birth?

Or how can we part indeed, the show, the portent, the sign,
From the simple words which glow with the light of a teaching Divine?

And if careless of these, as of growths which spring up and bear fruit and fall,
Yet how shall our thought accept the crowning wonder of all?

Yet if this we reject, wherein doth our faith and assurance lie?
What is it to us that God lives, we who live for a little and die;

Or why were it not more wise to live as the beasts of
    to-day,
Taking life, while it lasts, as a gift, and secure of the
    future as they?

Then the voice: Oh, disease of doubt! now I seem to
    hold you indeed,
Keeping fast in my grasp at length the sum of your
    dreary creed.

How else should man prove God's will, than through
    methods of human thought?
How else than through human words shall he gather the
    things that he ought?

If the Lord should speak day by day from Sinai, 'mid
    clouds and fire,
Should we hear 'mid those thunders loud the still voices
    which now inspire?

Would not either that awful sound, like that vivid and
    scorching blaze,
Confuse our struggling thought, and our tottering foot-
    steps amaze?

Or, if it should sound so clear that to hear were to obey indeed,
'Twere a thing of dry knowledge alone, not one of a faithful creed;

No lantern for erring feet, but a glare on a white, straight road,
Where life struggled its weary day, to sink before night with its load;

Where the blinded soul might long for the shade of a cloud of doubt,
And yearn for dead silence, to blot that terrible utterance out.

Yet God is not silent indeed; not seldom from every page—
From the lisping story of eld to the seer with his noble rage;

From the simple life divine, with its accents gentle and true,
To the thinker who formed by his learning and watered the faith as it grew:

All are fired by the Spirit of God. Nor true is the doubt you teach,
That God speaks not to all men the same, but differs 'twixt each and each.

Each differs from each a little, with difference of race and of clime;
Each is changed, but not transformed, with the onward process of time;

Each nation, each age, has its laws, whereto it shall stand or fall,
But built on a wider Law, which is under and over them all.

Nor doubt we that from Western wilds to the long-sealed isles of Japan,
There runs the unbroken realm of a Law that is common to man.

Not as ours shows the law they obey, and yet it is one and the same,
Though it comes in a varying shape, and is named by another name.

Not so shall your doubt prevail; nor if any should dream
    to-day,
By praise of Jew or of Greek, to dissolve His glory
    away,

Can they hold that God left His world with no gleam of
    glory from Him,
No light clouds edged with splendour, no radiance of
    Godhead dim.

Others were before Christ had come. Oh! dear dead
    Teacher, whose word,
Long before the sweet words on the Hill, young hearts
    had quickened and stirred;

Who spak'st of the soul and the life; with limbs chilled
    by the rising death,
Yielding up to thy faith, with a smile, the last gasp of
    thy earthly breath;—

And thou, oh golden-mouthed sage, who with brilliance
    of thought as of tongue,
Didst sing of thy Commonwealth fair, the noblest of
    epics unsung;

In whose pages thy Master's words shine forth, sublimed
    and refined
In the music of perfect language, inspired by a faithful
    mind ;—

And ye seers of Israel and doctors, whose breath was
    breathed forth to move
The dry dead bones of the Law with the life of a larger
    love ;—

Or thou, great Saint of the East, in whose footsteps the
    millions have trod
Till from life, like an innocent dream, they past and were
    lost in God ;—

And thou, quaint teacher of old, whose dead words,
    though all life be gone,
Through the peaceful Atheist realms keep the millions
    labouring on ;—

Shall I hold that ye, as the rest, spake no echo of things
    divine,
That no gleam of a clouded sun through the mists of
    your teaching may shine ?

Nay; such thoughts were to doubt of God. Yet, strange it is and yet sure,
No teacher of old was full of mercy as ours, or pure.

'Twixt the love that He taught, and the Greek with his nameless, terrible love,
Yawns a gulph as wide as parts, hell beneath and heaven above;

'Twixt His rule of a Higher Mercy and that which the Rabbi taught,
Lies the gulph between glowing Act and barren ashes of Thought.

For the pure thought smirched and fouled, or buried in pedant lore,
He brought a sweet Reason of Force, such as man knew never before.

What to us are the men of the East, though they preach their own Gospel indeed?
We are men of the West, and shall stand or fall by a Western creed.

Though we see in those Scriptures antique, faint flames of
    Diviner fire,
Who would change to Buddha from Christ, as a change
    from lower to higher?

Nay! He is our Teacher indeed. Little boots it to-day
    to seek
To arraign, with a laboured learning, the words that men
    heard Him speak;

To cavil, to carp, to strive, through the mists of an age-
    long haze,
To dim to a common light the star which could once
    amaze;

To fix by some pigmy canon, too short for the tale of
    to-day,
The facts of a brief life, fled eighteen centuries away;

To mark by a guess, and to spurn, as born of a later age,
The proofs which, whenever writ, bear God's finger on
    every page;

Or to sneer at the wonders they saw Him work, or believed they saw;
We who know that unbending sequence is only a phase of law,

No wonder which God might do if it rested on witness of men,
Would turn to it our thought of to-day as it turned the multitudes then.

Nor proved would avail a whit if the teaching itself were not pure;
Nor if it were pure as His would make it one whit more sure.

And for the great Wonder of all. If any there be who fears
That the spark of God in his breast may be quenched in a few short years;

Who feels his faith's fire blaze up more clear than it burnt before,
By the thought of the empty tomb and the stone rolled back from the door:

For him was the miracle done. If no proof makes clearer to me
Than His word to my inner sense, the Higher life that shall be;

If no Force that has once leapt forth can ever decline and fall,
From the dead forces stirring the worlds, to the Life-force which dominates all;

But the sum of life is the same, and shall be when the world is done,
As it was when its first faint spark was stirred by the kiss of the sun;—

If I feel a sure knowledge within, which shall never be blotted out,
A Longing, a Faith, a Conviction too strong for a Whisper of Doubt

That my life shall be hid with a Lord, who shall do the thing that is best—
To be purged, it may be, long time, or taken at once to rest,—

To live, it may be, myself; from all else, individual, sole,
Or blended with other lives, or sunk in the Infinite whole—

(Though I doubt not that that which is I may endure in the ages to be,
Since I know not what bars hold apart the Not-Me and the mystical Me ;—)

How else than thro' Him do I grasp the faith that for Greek and Jew
Was hidden, or but dimly seen, which nor Moses nor Socrates knew?

Ay! He is our Teacher indeed. He is risen, and we shall rise;
But if only as we He rose, not the less He lives in the skies.

And if those who proclaim Him to-day in the dim gray lands of the East,
Prove him not by portent or sign, not by trick or secret of priest;

But for old cosmogonies dead, and faint precepts too weak for our need,
Offer God brought nearer to man in a living and glowing creed.

The pure teaching, the passionate love, taking thought for the humble and weak,
The pitiful scorn of wrong which His Scriptures everywhere speak,

Not writ for the sage in his cell, but preached 'mid the turmoil and strife,
And touched with a living brand from the fire of the Altar of Life.

So, of all the wonders they tell, no wonder our hearts has stirred
Like the Wonder which lives with us still in a living and breathing Word.

More than portents, more than all splendours of rank loyal hearts devise,
More than visions of heavenly forms caught up and lost in the skies,

This the crowning miracle shows, before which we must
    prostrate fall ;
For this is the living voice of the Lord and Giver of all.

*   *   *   *   *

Then I ceased again from thought, as I lay on the long
    green grass,
Thrilled through by a music of hymns, and letting the
    moments pass.

Exult and rejoice ! they sang in high unison, now com-
    bined
Which were warring voices before, the voices of heart
    and mind.

The earth was flooded with light, over valley and river
    and hill,
And this is the hymn which I heard them sing, while the
    world lay still :

Exult, oh dust and ashes !   Rejoice, all ye that are
    dead !
For ye live too who lie beneath as we live who walk
    overhead.

As God lives, so ye are living; ye are living and moving to-day,
Not as they live who breathe and move, yet living and conscious as they.

And ye too, oh living, exult. Young and old, exult and rejoice;
For the Lord of the quick and the dead lives still: we have heard His voice.

We have heard His voice, and we hear it sound wider and more increased,
To the sunset plains of the West from the peaks of the furthest East.

For the quick and the dead, it was given; for them it is sounding still,
And no pause of silence shall break the clear voice of the Infinite Will.

Not only through Christ long since, and the teachers of ages gone,
But to-day He speaks, day by day, to those who are toiling on;

More clear perhaps then to the ear, and with nigher
    voice and more plain,
But still the same Teacher Divine, speaking to us again
    and again.

For I like not his creed, if any there be, who shall dare
    to hold
That God comes to us only at times far away in the
    centuries old.

Not so; but He dwells with us still; and maybe, though
    I know not indeed,
He will send us a Christ again, with a fuller and perfecter
    creed—

A Christ who shall speak to all men, East and West, and
    North and South,
Till the whole world shall hear and believe the gracious
    words of His mouth.

When knowledge has pierced through the wastes, chaining
    earth together and sea,
And the bars of to-day are lost in the union of all that
    shall be;

And the brotherhood that He loved is more than a saintly thought,
And the wars and the strifes which we mourn are lost in the peace He taught;

Then Christ coming shall make all things new. Or it may be that ages of pain
Shall quench the dim light of to-day, bringing back the thick darkness again.

And then, slow as the tide which flows on though each wave may seem to recede,
Man advances again and again to the Rock of a higher creed.

Or it may be no teacher shall come down again with God in his face,
But the light which before was reflected from One shall shine on the race.

And as this wide earth grows smaller, and men to men nearer draw,
There may spring from the root of the race the flower of a nobler law,

Growing fairer, and still more fair ; or maybe, through long ages of time,
Man shall rise up from type to type, to the strength of an essence sublime,

Removed as far in knowledge, in length of life, and in good,
From us as we from the mollusc which gasped in the first warm flood,—

A creature so wise and so high that he scorns all allurement of ill,
Marching on through an ordered life in the strength of a steadfast will.

Who knows? But, however it be, we live, and shall live indeed,
In ourselves or in others to come. What more doth our longing need?

Hid with God, or on earth, we shall see, burning brighter and yet more bright,
The sphere of humanity move throughout time on its pathway of light;

Circling round with a narrower orbit, as age upon age
    fleets away,
The centre of Force and of Being, the Fountain of Light
    and of Day,

Till, nearer drawn, and more near, at last it shall merge
    and fall.
In its source; man is swallowed in God, the Part is lost
    in the All;

One more world is recalled to rest, one more star adds its
    fire to the sun,
One light less wanders thro' space, and the story of man
    is done.

    *   *   *   *   *

Then slowly I rose to go from my place on the long green
    grass,
Where so long I had lain in deep thought, and letting
    the moments pass.

A great light was flooding all the plains of the earth and
    the sky,
The low church and the deep-sunk vale, and the place
    where one day I shall lie,

Evensong.

The fresh graves of those we have lost, the dark yews with their reverend gloom,
And the green wave which only marks the place of the nameless tomb;

And thro' all the clear spaces above—oh wonder! oh glory of Light!—
Came forth myriads on myriads of worlds, the shining host of the night,—

The vast forces and fires that know the same sun and centre as we;
The faint planets which roll in vast orbits round suns we shall never see;

The rays which had sped from the first, with the awful swiftness of light,
To reach only then, it might be, the confines of mortal sight.

Oh, wonder of cosmical order! oh, Maker and Ruler of all,
Before whose Infinite greatness in silence we worship and fall!

Could I doubt that the Will which keeps this great universe steadfast and sure
Can be less than His creatures thought, full of goodness,
 pitiful, pure?

Could I dream that the Power which keeps those great
 suns circling around,
Takes no thought for the humblest life which flutters and
 falls to the ground?

Oh, Faith! thou art higher than all. Then I turned
 from the glories above,
And from every casement new-lit there shone a soft
 radiance of love.

Young mothers were teaching their children to fold little
 hands in prayer;
Strong fathers were resting from toil, 'mid the hush of the
 Sabbath air.

Peasant lovers strolled thro' the lanes, shy and diffident,
 each with each,
Yet knit by some subtle union too fine for their halting
 speech.

Humble lives, to low thought, and low ; but linked, to
    the thinker's eye,
By a bond that is stronger than death, with the lights of
    the farthest sky.

Here as there, the great drama of life rolled on, and a
    jubilant voice
Thrilled through me ineffable, vast, and bade me exult
    and rejoice.

Exult and rejoice, oh soul ! sang my being to a
    mystical hymn
As I passed by the cool bright wolds, as I threaded my
    pinewoods dim ;

Rejoice and be sure ! as I passed to my fair home
    under the hill,
Wrapt round with a happy content,—and the world
    and my soul were still.

SONG.

Beam on me, fair Ideal, beam on me!
   Too long thou hast concealed thee in a cloud;
Mine is no vision strong to pierce to thee,
   Nor voice complaining loud,
Whereby thou mightest find thy dear, and come
To thine own heart, and long expecting home.

Too long thou dost withdraw thee from mine eyes;
   Too long thou lingerest. Ah, truant sweet!
Dost thou no reckoning take of all my sighs,
   While Time with flying feet
Speeds onward, till the westering sun sinks low—
With cruel feet so swift and yet so slow?

Time was I thought that thou wouldst come a maid
   White-armed, with deep blue eyes and sunny head;
But, ah! too long the lovely vision stayed.
   And then, when this was fled,
Fame, with blown clarion clear, and wide-spread wings,
Fame, crown and summit of created things.

And then in guise of Truth, when this grew faint,
　　Truth in Belief and Act, and Life and Thought,
White-robed and virginal, a pure cold saint,
　　Thou camest a while, long sought ;
But only in glimpses camest thou, so I
Watch wearily until thou passest by.

I wait, I watch, I hunger, though I know
　　Thou wilt not come at all who stay'st so long.
My hope has lost its strength, my heart its glow ;
　　I grow too cold for song :
Long since I might have sung, hadst thou come then,
A song to echo through the souls of men.

Yet, since 'tis better far to dream in sleep,
　　Than wholly lose the treacheries of time,
I hold it gain to have seen thy garments sweep
　　On the far hills sublime :
Still will I hope thy glorious face to see,—
Beam on me, fair Ideal, beam on me !

———o———

AT LAST.

LET me at last be laid
On that hillside I know which scans the vale,
Beneath the thick yews' shade,
For shelter when the rains and winds prevail.
It cannot be the eye
Is blinded when we die,
So that we know no more at all
The dawns increase, the evenings fall;
Shut up within a rotting chest of wood,
Asleep, and careless of our children's good.

Shall I not feel the spring,
The yearly resurrection of the earth,
Stir thro' each sleeping thing
With the fair throbbings and alarms of birth,
Calling at its own hour
On folded leaf and flower,
Calling the lamb, the lark, the bee,
Calling the crocus and anemone,
Calling new lustre to the maiden's eye,
And to the youth love and ambition high?

At Last.

Shall I no more admire
The winding river kiss the daisied plain?
Nor see the dawn's cold fire
Steal downward from the rosy hills again?
Nor watch the frowning cloud,
Sublime with mutterings loud,
Burst on the vale, nor eves of gold,
Nor crescent moons, nor starlight cold,
Nor the red casements glimmer on the hill
At Yule-tides, when the frozen leas are still?

Or should my children's tread
Through Sabbath twilights, when the hymns are done,
Come softly overhead,
Shall no sweet quickening through my bosom run,
Till all my soul exhale
Into the primrose pale,
And every flower which springs above
Breathes a new perfume from my love;
And I shall throb, and stir, and thrill beneath
With a pure passion stronger far than death?

Sweet thought! fair, gracious dream,
Too fair and fleeting for our clearer view!

How should our reason deem
That those dear souls, who sleep beneath the blue
In rayless caverns dim,
'Mid ocean monsters grim,
Or whitening on the trackless sand,
Or with strange corpses on each hand
In battle-trench or city graveyard lie,
Break not their prison-bonds till time shall die?

Nay, 'tis not so indeed.
With the last fluttering of the failing breath
The clay-cold form doth breed
A viewless essence, far too fine for death;
And ere one voice can mourn,
On upward pinions borne,
They are hidden, they are hidden, in some thin air,
Far from corruption, far from care,
Where through a veil they view their former scene,
Only a little touched by what has been.

Touched but a little; and yet,
Conscious of every change that doth befal,
By constant change beset,
The creatures of this tiny whirling ball,

At Last.

Filled with a higher being,
Dowered with a clearer seeing,
Risen to a vaster scheme of life,
To wider joys and nobler strife,
Viewing our little human hopes and fears
As we our children's fleeting smiles and tears.

Then, whether with fire they burn
This dwelling-house of mine when I am fled,
And in a marble urn
My ashes rest by my beloved dead,
Or in the sweet cold earth
I pass from death to birth,
And pay kind Nature's life-long debt
In heart's-ease and in violet—
In charnel-yard or hidden ocean wave,
Where'er I lie, I shall not scorn my grave.

———o———

A MEMORIAL.

White marbles, treasures of the mine,
    Fair carvings round a jewelled cross,
Adorn the delicate golden shrine
    Where love commemorates its loss.

Thus England strives to glorify
    One whose fine nature blended here
The artist hand, the seeing eye,
    The high musician's subtle ear.

Around him groups each useful art
    Which gives us covering, shelter, food;
Which knits the nations thrust apart;
    Which smoothes the hill, or spans the flood.

And, in the fair relief which runs
    Around the high-set basement, stand,
Each in the noblest of her sons
    The royal arts of brain and hand.

A Memorial.

Homer and Shakspeare, Kings of Song;
    Mozart and Handel, Lords of Sound;
Phidias; and Angelo, the strong;
    Sweet Raphael, throned with painters round.

While, at the broad base, carven white,
    Like sentinels on either hand,
Symbolic to the finer sight,
    The great Earth's four divisions stand.

Her strong bull, Europe seems to ride;
    Asia, her huge obedient beast;—
With queens of fancy on each side;—
    With eagle faces of the East.

Afric, with kneeling camel mild;
    And broad-lipped Nubian, swart of hue;
Columbia, keen, with bison wild;
    Indian; and Inca of Peru.

And, canopied within the shrine,
    Gazing with contemplative eyes,
The comely form and features fine
    Of one who was as good as wise.

Who spent what intervals were his,
   From graver duties of the State,
Not in the silken frivolous ease
   And laboured leisure of the great:

Nor walked with those who cared for nought
   But how the careless hours to fill,
Nor any joy of act or thought
   Nought but to game, and dance, and kill.

These drew him not, whose happy home
   Filled every thought; who knew the love
Of a true wife, and children come,
   His tenderness and love to move.

And rested there with Art and Song,
   Science and Thought,—a glorious quire,
And Love, the Master-Player, strong
   To wake each separate chord with fire.

A thousand homes like his there be
   In this our happy, peaceful land;
But none set high for all to see,
   Nor girt by watchers on each hand.

Nor yet so gracious and refined
    As is the stately life of Kings,
Who, safe from every ruder wind,
    See Time fleet by on noiseless wings.

A Royal home! In all the life
    Of England came not days like these;
Stern days of war and civil strife;
    Soft days of sensual sloth and ease;

All these were hers. But this had come
    Never at all, this ordered life,
This finer and more gracious home
    Built on the hearts of man and wife,

Till this man came. Let those who know
    What perils compass round a throne,
What fierce temptations burn and glow
    Round one who lives and breathes alone,

Think it more honour to have been
    So pure, that never slander's breath
Touched the first subject of his Queen,
    Blameless in life, bewailed in death,

Than to have ranged in peaceful strife
    The gathered fruit of brain and hand,
And drawn the precious arts of life
    Together from every distant land,

Till under those long aisles of glass
    Men thronged, and dreamt the end of war—
Nor, tho' Time mocks our hopes, alas!
    Deem we since then the change so far,—

Higher than this, or to have led
    Our rugged English mind and heart
To love the mighty Masters, dead,
    Who live in every living Art.

Or, with wise kindness, to have sought
    The seeker, who elects to take
No other riches than his thought,
    Counting all gain for knowledge sake.

Most precious deeds, and fit to earn
    What record loving hearts devise;
High monument, and words that burn,
    But, more than all of them, we prize

Exceeding these as it exceeds
   The fame of warriors strong to kill;
Ay, even the statesman's thoughts and deeds,
   Which sway the docile nation's will.

The high example, white and pure;
   The fair life, dutiful and mild;
The loving thought, which shall endure
   Beyond the love of wife and child.

Rest, happy shade! within the shrine
   Thy Love has built, securely rest;
And teach, from out thy calm divine,
   Peoples and Kings what life is best.

———o———

SONG.

Love-sighs that are sighed and spent in vain,
Ah! folly, folly,
Thou dost transmute into a precious pain,
Sweet melancholy.
Ah! folly, folly,
Ah! fair melancholy,
Sweeter by far thy mild remedial pain,
Than if fierce hope should rise and throb again.

High hopes of glory sunk to nought,
Ah! folly, folly,
And deep perplexities of baffled thought
Thou healest, melancholy.
Ah! folly, folly,
Ah! sweet melancholy,
Thou dost bear with thee a balm unsought,
To heal the wounds of love and pride and thought.

Yet thou art a trivial cure for ill,
Pale melancholy,
Fitting best a feebler brain and will,
Ah ! folly, folly.
Ay, sweet melancholy
Folly art thou, folly.
Who only may not trivial ills endure
Will in thy pharmacy repose his cure.

Since thou shalt not heal the wounds I know,
Pale melancholy,
I will seek if any comfort grow
In jovial folly,
Ah ! folly, folly,
Worse than melancholy,
No other cure there is for Fortune's smart
Than a soul self-contained, and a proud innocent heart.

THE DIALOGUE.

UNTO my soul I said,
 "Oh, vagrant soul!
When o'er my living head
 A few years roll,
Is't true that thou shalt fly
Far away into the sky,
Leaving me in my place
Alone with my disgrace?

For thou wilt stand in the East,
 The night withdrawn,
White-robed as is a priest,
 At the door of dawn;
While I within the ground,
In misery fast bound,
Shall lie, blind, deaf, and foul,
Since thou art fled, O soul."

Then said my soul to me:
 "Thy lot is best;
For thou shalt tranquil be,
 Sunk deep in rest,

The Dialogue.

While naked I shall know
The intolerable glow
When as, the sun, shall rise
A fire in fiery skies.

Thou shalt lie cool and dark,
    Forgetting all ;
I shall float shamed and stark,
    Till the sun fall.
Thou shalt be earth in earth,
Preparing for new birth ;
While me in the heaven fierce,
Pure glories fright and pierce."

Then said I to my soul,
    And she to me :
"Where'er life's current roll
    We twain shall be,
Part here and part not here,
Partners in hope and fear,
Until, our exile done,
We meet at last in one."

THE BIRTH OF VERSE.

BLIND thoughts which occupy the brain,
    Dumb melodies which fill the ear,
Dim perturbations, precious pain,
    A gleam of hope, a chill of fear,—
These seize the poet's soul, and mould
The ore of fancy into gold.

And first no definite thought there is
    In all that affluence of sound,
Like those sweet formless melodies
    Piped to the listening woods around,
By birds which never teacher had
But love and knowledge: they are glad.

Till, when the chambers of the soul
    Are filled with inarticulate airs,
A spirit comes which doth control
    The music, and its end prepares;
And, with a power serene and strong,
Shapes these wild melodies to song.

Or haply, thoughts which glow and burn
    Await long time the fitting strain,

Which, swiftly swelling, seems to turn
    The silence to a load of pain ;
And somewhat in him seems to cry,
"I will have utterance, or I die!"

Then of a sudden, full, complete,
    The strong strain bursting into sound,
Words come with rhythmic rush of feet,
    Fit music girds the language round,
And with a sweetness all unsought
Soars up the winged embodied thought.

But howsoever they may rise,
    Fit words and music come to birth;
There soars an angel to the skies,
    There walks a Presence on the earth—
A something which shall yet inspire
Myriads of souls unborn with fire.

And when his voice is hushed and dumb,
    The flame burnt out, the glory dead,
He feels a thrill of wonder come
    At that which his poor tongue has said ;
And thinks of each diviner line—
"Only the hand that wrote was mine."

FROM HADES.

IN February, when the dawn was slow,
And winds lay still, I gazed upon the fields
Which stretched before me lifeless, and the stream
Which laboured in the distance to the sea,
Sullen and cold. No force of fancy took
My thought to bloomy June, when all the land
Was deep in crested grass, and through the dew
The landrail brushed, and the lush banks were set
With strawberries, and the hot noise of bees
Lulled the bright flowers. Rather I seemed to move
Thro' that weird land, Hellenic fancy feigned,
Beyond the fabled river and the bark
Of Charon; and forthwith on every side
Rose the thin throng of ghosts.
       And first I saw
A manly hunter pace along the lea,
His bow upon his shoulders, and his spear
Poised idly in his hand : the face and form
Of vigorous youth; but in the full brown eyes
A timorous gaze as of a hunted hart,

Brute-like, yet human still, even as the Faun
Of old, the dumb brute passing into man,
And dowered with double nature. As he came
I seemed to question of his fate, and he
Answered me thus:
     " 'Twas one hot afternoon
That I, a hunter, wearied with my day,
Heard my hounds baying fainter on the hills,
Led by the flying hart; and when the sound
Faded and all was still, I turned to seek,
O'ercome by heat and thirst, a little glade,
Deep in the cool recesses of the wood,
Where the cold crystal of a mossy pool
Rose to the flowery marge, and gave again
The soft green lawn where ofttimes, overspent,
I lay upon the grass and eager bathed
My limbs in the clear lymph.
      But as I neared
The hollow, sudden through the leaves I saw
A throng of wood-nymphs fair, sporting undraped
Round one, a goddess. She with timid hand
Loosened her zone, and glancing round let fall
Her robe from neck and bosom, pure and bright,
(For it was Dian's self: I saw none else)

As when she frees her from a fleece of cloud
And swims along the deep blue sea of heaven
On sweet June nights. Silent awhile I stood,
Rooted with awe, and fain had turned to fly,
But feared by careless footstep to affright
Those chaste cold eyes. Great awe and reverence
Held me, and fear; then Love with passing wing
Fanned me, and held my eyes, and checked my breath,
Signing 'Beware!'
     So for a time I watched,
Breathless as one a brooding nightmare holds,
Who fleeth some great fear, yet fleeth not,
Till the last flutter of lawn, and veil no more
Obscured, and all the beauty of my dreams
Assailed my sense; but ere I raised my eyes,
As one who fain would look and see the sun,
The first glance dazed my brain. Only I knew
The perfect outline flow in tender curves,
To break in double beauties; only a haze
Of creamy white, dimple, and deep divine:
And then no more. For lo! a sudden chill,
And such thick mist as shuts the hills at eve,
Oppressed me gazing; and a heaven-sent shame,
An awe, a fear, a reverence for the unknown,

From Hades.

Froze all the springs of will and left me cold,
And blinded all the longings of my eyes,
Leaving such dim reflection still as mocks
Him who has looked on a great light, and keeps
On his closed eyes the image.   Presently,
Hidden as Eve hid her, 'mid the dewy groves
Of Paradise, my fainting soul renewed
And straight, the innocent brute within the man
Bore on me, and with half-averted mind
I gazed upon the secret.
     As I looked
A radiance white, as beamed the frosty moon
On the mad boy and slew him, beamed on me;
Made chill my pulses, checked my life and heat;
Transformed me, withered all my soul, and left
My being burnt out.   For lo ! the dreadful eyes
Of Godhead met my gaze, and through the mask
And thick disguise of sense, as through a wood,
Pierced to my life.   Then suddenly I knew
An altered nature, touched by no desire
For that which showed so lovely, but declined
To lower levels.   Nought of fear or awe,
Nothing of love was mine.   Wide-eyed I gazed,
But saw no spiritual beam to blight

My brain with too much beauty, no undraped
And awful majesty; only a brute,
Dumb charm, like that which draws the brute to it,
Unknowing it is drawn. So gradually
I knew a dull content o'ercloud my sense,
And unabashed I gazed, like that dumb bird
Which thinks no thought and speaks no word, yet fronts
The sun that blinded Homer—all my fear
Sunk with my shame, in a base happiness.

But as I gazed, and careless turned and passed
Through the thick wood, forgetting what had been,
And thinking thoughts no longer, swift there came
A mortal terror: voices that I knew,
My own hounds' bayings that I loved before,
As with them often o'er the purple hills
I chased the flying hart from slope to slope,
Before the slow sun climbed the Eastern peaks,
Until the swift sun smote the Western plains;
Whom often I had cheered by voice and word,
Whom often I had checked with hand and thong;—
Grim followers, like the passions, firing me;
True servants, like the strong nerves, urging me
On many a fruitless chase, to find and take

From Hades.

Some too swift-fleeting beauty; faithful feet
And tongues, obedient always. These I knew,
Clothed with a new-born force and vaster grown,
And stronger than their master; and I thought,
What if they tare me with their jaws, nor knew
That once I ruled them,—brute pursuing brute,
And I the quarry? Then I turned and fled,—
If it was I indeed that feared and fled—
Down the long glades, and through the tangled brakes,
Where scarce the sunlight pierced; fled on and on,
And panted, self-pursued. But evermore
The dissonant music which I knew so sweet,
When on the windy hills, and vales deep-set,
And whispering pines it came; now far, now near,
As from my rushing steed I leant and cheered
With voice and horn the chase, this brought to me
Fear of I knew not what, which bade me fly,
Fly always, fly; but when my heart stood still,
And all my limbs were stiffened as I fled,
Just as the white moon ghost-like climbed the sky,
Nearer they came and nearer, baying loud,
With bloodshot eyes and red jaws dripping foam;
And when I strove to check their savagery,
Speaking with words; no voice articulate came,

Only a dumb, low bleat. Then all the throng
Leapt swift on me, and tore me as I lay,
And left me man again.
      Wherefore I walk
Along these dim fields peopled with the ghosts
Of heroes who have left the ways of earth
For this faint ghost of them. Sometimes I think,
Pondering on what has been, that all my days
Were shadows, all my life an allegory;
And, though I know sometimes some fainter gleam
Of the old beauty move me, and sometimes
Some beat of the old pulses, that my life,
For ever hurrying on in hot pursuit,
To fall at length self-slain, was but a tale
Writ large by Zeus upon a mortal life,
Writ large, and yet a riddle; for sometimes
I read its meaning thus : Life is a chase,
And man the hunter, always chasing on,
With hounds of rushing thought or fiery sense,
Some hidden truth or beauty, fleeting on
For ever through the thick-leaved coverts vast
And wind-worn wolds of life. And if we turn
A moment from the hot pursuit to seize
Some chance-brought sweetness, other than the search

To which our life is set,—some dalliance,
Some outward shape of Art, some lower love,
Some charm of wealth and sleek content and home,—
Then, if we check an instant, the swift chase
Of fierce untempered energies which pursue,
With jaws unsated and a thirst for life,
Bears down on us with clanging shock, and whelms
Our prize and us in ruin.   And sometimes
I seem to myself a thinker, who at last,
By some dark lake of thought unknown, unseen,
Amid the chase and capture of low ends,
Comes one day on some perfect truth, and looks
Till the fair vision blinds him heart and brain,
And, all his former nature hurrying on,
The strong brute forces and unchecked desires,
Finding him bound and speechless, think him now
No more their master, but some soulless thing;
And leap on him, and seize him, and possess
His life, till through death's gate he pass to life,
And his own ghost revives.   But looks no more
Upon the truth unveiled, but through a cloud
Of creed and faith and longing, which shall change
One day to perfect knowledge.

　　　　　　　　　　But whoe'er
Shall read the riddle of my life, I walk
In this dim land amid dim ghosts of kings,
As one day thou shalt; meantime, fare thou well."

Then passed he; and I marked him slowly go
Along the winding ways of that dim land,
And vanish in a wood.
　　　　　　　　Sudden I saw
Two who together walked : one with a lyre
Of gold, which gave no sound ; the other hung
Upon his breast, and closely clung to him,
Spent in a tender longing.　As they came,
I heard her gentle voice recounting o'er
Some ancient tale, and these the words she said :
" Dear voice and lyre now silent, which I heard
Across yon sullen river, bringing to me
All my old life, and he, the ferryman,
Heard and obeyed, and the grim monster heard
And fawned on you.　Joyous thou camest and free
Like a white sunbeam from the dear bright earth,
Where suns shone clear, and moons beamed bright, and
　　　streams

Laughed with a rippling music (nor as here
The dumb stream stole, the veiled sky slept, the fields
Were lost in twilight). Like a morning breeze,
Which blows in summer from the gates of dawn
Across the fields of spice, and wakes to life
Their slumbering perfume, through this silent land
Where scarce a footstep sounds, nor any strain
Of earthly song, you came; and suddenly
The pale cheeks flushed a little, the murmured words
Rose to a faint, thin treble; the throng of ghosts
Pacing along the sunless ways and still,
Felt a new life. Thou camest, dear, and straight
The dull cold river broke in sparkling foam,
The pale and scentless flowers grew perfumed; last
To the dim chamber, where with the sad queen
I sat in gloom, and silently inwove
Dead wreaths of amaranths; thy music came
Laden with life, and I, who seemed to know
Not life's voice only, but my own, rose up,
Along the hollow pathways following
The sound which brought back earth and life and love,
And memory and longing. Yet I went
With half-reluctant footsteps, as of one
Whom passion draws, or some high fantasy,

Despite himself, because some subtle spell,
Part born of dread to cross that sullen stream
And its grim guardians, part of secret shame
Of the young airs and freshness of the earth,
Being that I was, enchained me.

                        "Then at last,
From voice and lyre so high a strain arose
As trembled on the utter verge of being,
And thrilling, poured out life. Thus closelier drawn
I walked with thee, shut in by halcyon sound
And soft environments of harmony,
Beyond the ghostly gates, beyond the dim
Calm fields, where the beetle hummed and the pale owl
Stole noiseless from the copse, and the white blooms
Stetched thin for lack of sun : so fair a light
Born out of consonant sound environed me.
Nor looked I backward, as we seemed to move
To some high goal of thought and life and love,
Like twin birds flying fast with equal wing
Out of the night, to meet the coming sun
Above a sea. But on thy dear fair eyes,
The eyes that well I knew on the old earth,
I looked not, for with still averted gaze
Thou leddest, and I followed ; for, indeed,

While that high strain was sounding, I was rapt
In faith and a high courage, driving out
All doubt and discontent and womanish fear,
Nay, even my love itself. But when awhile
It sunk a little, or seemed to sink and fall
To lower levels, seeing that use makes blunt
The too accustomed ear, straightway desire
To look once more on thy recovered eyes
Seized me, and oft I called with piteous voice,
Beseeching thee to turn. But thou long time
Wert even as one who heard not, with grave sign
And waving hand denying. Finally,
When now we neared the stream, on whose far shore
Lay life, great terror took me, and I shrieked
Thy name, as in despair. Then thou, as one
Who knows him set in some great jeopardy,
A swift death fronting him on either hand,
Didst slowly turning gaze; and lo! I saw
Thine eyes grown awful, life that looked on death,
Clear purity on dark and cankered sin,
The immortal on corruption,—not the eyes
That erst I knew in life, but dreadfuller
And stranger; as I looked, I seemed to swoon,
Some blind force whirled me back, and when I woke

I saw thee vanish in the middle stream,
A speck on the dull waters, taking with thee
My life, and leaving Love with me. But I
Not for myself bewail, but all for thee,
Who, but for me, wert now among the stars
With thy great Lord; I sitting at thy feet.
But now the fierce and unrestrained band
Of passions woman-natured, finding thee
Scornful of love within thy Thracian cave,
With blind rage falling on thee, tore thy limbs,
And left thee to the Muses' sepulture,
While thy soul dwells in Hades; but I wail
My weakness always, who for Love destroyed
The life that was my Love. I prithee, dear,
Forgive me if thou canst, who hast lost heaven
To save a loving woman."
      He with voice
Sweeter than any mortal melody,
And plaintive as the music that is made
By the Æolian strings, or the sad bird
That sings of summer nights:
       "Eurydice,
Dear love, be comforted; not once alone
That which thou mournest haps, but day by day

Some lonely soul which walks apart and feeds
On high hill pastures, far from the herds of men,
Comes to the low fat fields, and sunny vales
Joyous with fruits and flowers, and the white arms
Of laughing love; and there awhile he stays
Content, forgetting all the joys he knew,
When first the morning breaks upon the hills,
And the keen air breathes from the Eastern gates
Like a pure draught of wine; forgetting all
The strains which float, as from a nearer heaven,
To him who treads at dawn the untrodden snows,
While all the warm world sleeps;—forgetting these,
And all things that have been. And if he gain
To raise to his own heights the simpler souls
That dwell upon the plains, the untutored thought,
The museless lives, the unawakened brain
That yet might soar, then is he blest indeed.
But if he fail, then leaving love behind,
The wider love of the race, the closer love
Of some congenial soul, he turns again
To the old difficult heights, and there alone
Dwells, till the widowed passions of his heart
Tear him and rend his soul, and drive him down
To the low plains he left. And there he dwells,

Missing the sky, dearest, and the white peaks,
And the light air of old; but in their stead
Finding the soft sweet sun of the vale, the clouds
Which veil the heavens indeed, but give the rains
That feed the streams of life and make earth green,
And bring at last the harvest. So I walk
In this dim land content with thee, O Love,
Untouched by any yearning of regret
For those old days; nor that the lyre which made
Erewhile such potent music now is dumb;
Nor that the voice which once could move the earth
(Zeus speaking through it), speaks in household words
Of homely love : Love is enough for me
With thee, O dearest; and perchance at last,
Zeus willing, this dumb lyre and whispered voice
Shall wake, by Love inspired, to such high note
As mounts above the stars, and swelling takes
Our souls to highest heaven."

       Then he stooped,
And, folded in one long embrace, they went
And faded in the darkness.

         Presently
One other ghost I saw, a comely boy,
With lip and cheek just touched with manly down,

And strong limbs wearing spring, in mien and garb
A youthful chieftain, with a perfect face
Of fresh young beauty, clustered curls divine,
And chiselled features like a sculptured god,
But warm and breathing life; only the eyes,
The fair large eyes, were full of dreaming thought,
And seemed to gaze beyond the world of sight,
On a hid world of beauty. Him I stayed,
Accosting with soft words of courtesy;
And, on a bank of scentless flowers reclined,
He answered thus:

    "Not for the garish sun
I long, nor for the splendours of high noon
In this dim land I languish; for I mind
How ofttimes when the swift chase swept along
Through the brisk morn, or when my comrades stript
For wrestling, or the foot-race, or to cleave
The sunny stream, I loved to walk apart,
Self-centred, sole; and when the laughing girls
To some fair stripling's oaten melody
Made ready for the dance, I heeded not;
Nor when to the loud trumpet's blast and blare
My peers rode forth to battle. For, one eve,
In Latmos, after a long day in June,

I stayed to rest me on a wooded hill,
Where often youth and maid were wont to meet
Toward moonrise ; and deep slumber fell on me.
Thinking of Love, just as the ruddy orb
Rose on the lucid night, set in a frame
Of myrtle and of sharp plane tremulous,
Deep slumber fell, and loosed my limbs in rest.

Then, as the full orb poised upon the peak,
There came a beauteous vision of a maid,
Who seemed to step as from a golden car
Out of the low-hung moon. No mortal form,
Such as ofttimes of yore I knew and clasped
At twilight 'mid the vines at the mad feast
Of Dionysus, or the fair maids cold
Who streamed in white processions to the shrine
Of the chaste Virgin Goddess; but a shape
Richer and yet more pure. No thinnest veil
Obscured her ; but each exquisite limb revealed,
Gleamed like a golden statue subtly wrought
By a great sculptor on the architrave
Of some high temple vast—only in her
Each limb was soft and warm, and charged with life
And breathing. As I seemed to gaze on her,

From Hades.

Nearer she drew and gazed; and as I lay
Supine, as in a spell, the radiance stooped
And kissed me on the lips, a chaste, sweet kiss,
Which drew my spirit with it. So I slept
Each night upon the hill, until the dawn
Came in her silver chariot from the East,
And chased my Love away; but ever thus
Dissolved in love as in a heaven-sent dream,
Whenever the bright circle of the moon
Rose on the hills, whether in leafy June
Or harvest-tide, or when they leapt and pressed
Red-thighed the spouting must, I walked apart
From all, and took no thought for mortal maid,
Nor nimble joys of youth; but night by night
I stole, when all were sleeping, to the hill,
And slumbered and was blest; until I grew
Possest by love so deep, I seemed to live
In slumbers only, while the waking day
Showed faint as any vision.
                         So I turned
Paler and paler with the months, and climbed
The steep with laboured steps and difficult breath,
But still I climbed. Ay, though the wintry frost
Chained fast the streams and whitened every hill,

I sought my mistress through the leafless groves,
And slumbered and was happy, till the dawn
Returning found me stretched out, cold and stark,
With life's fire nigh burnt out. Till one clear night,
When the birds shivered in the pines, and all
The inner heavens stood open, lo! she came,
Brighter and kinder still, and kissed my eyes
And half-closed lips, and drew my soul through them,
And in one precious ecstasy dissolved
My life. And thenceforth ever on the hill
I lie unseen of man, a cold, white form,
Still young, through all the ages; but my soul,
Clothed in this thin presentment of old days,
Walks this dim land, where never moonrise comes,
Nor day-break, but a twilight waiting-time.
No more; and, ah! how weary! Yet I judge
My lot a higher far than his who spends
His youth on swift hot pleasure, quickly past;
Or those, my equals, who through long calm years
Grew sleek in dull content of wedded lives
And fair-grown offspring. Many a day for them,
While I was wandering here, and my bones bleached
Upon the hills, the sweet soft sun of June
Broke, and the grapes grew purple. Many a day

They heaped up gold, they knelt at festivals,
They waxed in high report and fame of men,
They gave their girls in marriage; while for me
Upon the untrodden peaks, the cold grey morn,
The snows, the rains, the winds, the untempered blaze,
Beat year by year, until I turned to stone,
And the great eagles shrieked at me, and wheeled
Affrighted. Yet I judge it best indeed
To seek in life, as now I know I sought,
Some fair impossible Love, which slays our life,
Some high ideal raised too high for man ;
And failing to grow mad, and cease to be,
Than to decline, as they do who have found
Broad-paunched content and weal and happiness;
And so an end. For one day, as I know,
The high aim unfulfilled fulfils itself;
The deep, unsatisfied thirst is satisfied ;
And through this twilight, broken suddenly,
The inmost heaven, the lucent stars of God,
The Moon of Love, the Sun of Life ; and I,
I who pine here—I on the Latmian hill
Shall soar aloft and find them."
       With the word,
The faint sun shot a beam athwart the fields,

And woke them, and the thrush from out the yew
Sang out reveillé to the coming day,
Soldier-like ; and the pomp and rush of life
Chased those young ghosts of time, and left me there,
A modern in the old age of the world.

SONG.

Oh! were I rich and mighty,
With store of gems and gold,
And you, a beggar at my gate,
Lay starving in the cold;
I wonder, could I bear
To leave you pining there?

Or, if I were an angel,
And you an earth-born thing,
Beseeching me to touch you
In rising with my wing;
I wonder should I soar
Aloft, nor heed you more?

Or, dear, if I were only
A maiden cold and sweet,
And you, a humble lover,
Sighed vainly at my feet;
I wonder if my heart
Would know no pain or smart?

THE ENIGMA.

THE gaslights flutter and flare
    On the cruel stones of the street,
And beneath in the sordid glare
    Pace legions of weary feet;
Fair faces that soon shall grow hard,
    Shy glances already grown bold,
The wrecks of a girlhood marred
    By shame and hunger and cold.

But here, as she passes along,
    Is one whose young cheek still shows,
'Mid the pallid, pitiful throng,
    The fresh bloom of a tender rose.
Not long has she walked with vice,
    A recruit to the army of Ill,
A fresh lamb for the sacrifice
    That steams up to Moloch still.

And the spell through which youth draws all,
  The faint shyness in hurrying walk,
The lithe form slender and tall,
  The soft burr in her simple talk,
Constrains the grave passer, whose brain
  Is long leagues of fancy apart,
To thrill with a sudden pain
  And an emptiness of heart.

Poor child ! since it is not long
  Since you were indeed but a child,
A gay thing of bird-like song,
  And even as a bird is wild ;
With no shadow of thought or care,
  Laughing all the sweet hours away,
When every morning was fair,
  And every season a May.

Through the red fallow on the hill
  The white team laboured along,
While you roamed the green copses at will,
  And mimicked the cuckoo's song ;

While they tossed and carried the hay,
    While the reapers were hid in the wheat,
You had only to laugh and to play,
    Or to bathe in the brook your feet.

For your mother left you a child,
    Your rough father's pride and joy:
Rejoiced that his girl was as wild
    And fearless as any boy.
Though you would not plunder the nest,
    Nor harry the shrieking hare,
You could gallop bare-backed with the best,
    And knew where the orchises were.

" Like a boy " was what they said,
    With your straight limbs and fearless face;
Like a girl in the golden head,
    Gay fancies, and nameless grace.
Like a boy in high courage and all
    Quick forces, and daring of will;
Like a girl in the peril to fall,
    And innocent blindness to ill.

And even now, on the sordid street,
    As you pass by the theatre door,
You bring with you some freshness sweet
    Of the brightness and breezes of yore.
Not yet are the frank eyes grown bold,
    Not yet have they lost all their joy;
Not yet has time taken the gold
    From the short crisp curls of the boy.

And if truly a boy's they were,
    Not thus would he pace forlorn;
Nor would careless passers-by dare
    To shoot out the lips of scorn.
Is it Nature or man that makes
    An unequal judgment arraign
Those whose equal nature takes
    The mark of the self-same stain?

Leaving this one shame and disgrace;
    Leaving that one honour and fame;
To this one confusion of face,
    To that one a stainless name:

A high port and respect and wealth
    For the one who is guilty indeed,
While the innocent walks by stealth
    Through rough places with feet that bleed.

Do I touch a deep ulcer of Time,
    A created or ultimate ill,
A primal curse or a crime,
    Self-inflicted through ignorance still?
But meanwhile, poor truant, you come
    With a new face year after year,
Leaving innocence, freedom, and home
    For these dens of weeping and fear.

To decline by a swift decay,
    To a thing so low and forlorn,
That, for all your fresh beauty to-day,
    It were better you never were born;
Or to find in some rare-sent hour,
    As a lily rooted in mire,
Love spring with its pure white flower
    From the lowest depths of desire.

The Enigma.

Heaven pity you ! So little turns
   The stream of our lives from the right;
So like is the flame that burns
   To the hearth that gives warmth and light;
So fine the impassable fence,
   Set for ever 'twixt right and wrong,
Between white lives of innocence
   And dark lives too dreadful for song.

TO THE TORMENTORS.

Dear little friend, who, day by day,
Before the door of home
Art ready waiting till thy master come,
With monitory paw and noise,
Swelling to half delirious joys,
Whether my path I take
By leafy coverts known to thee before,
Where the gay coney loves to play,
Or the loud pheasant whirls from out the brake
Unharmed by us, save for some frolic chase,
Or innocent panting race;
Or who, if by the sunny river's side
Haply my steps I turn,
With loud petition constantly dost yearn
To fetch the whirling stake from the warm tide;
Who, if I chide thee, grovellest in the dust,
And dost forgive me, though I am unjust,
Blessing the hand that smote; who with fond love
Gazest, and fear for me, such as doth move

To the Tormentors.

Those finer souls which know, yet may not see,
And are wrapped round and lost in ecstasy;—

And thou, dear little friend and soft,
Breathing a gentle air of hearth and home;
Whose low purr to the lonely ear doth oft
With deep refreshment come;
Though thy quick nature is not frank and gay
As that one's, yet with graceful play
Thou dost beguile the evenings, and dost sit
With mien demurely fit;
With half-closed eyes, as in a dream
Responsive to the singing steam,
Most delicately clean and white,
Thou baskest in the flickering light;
Quick-tempered art thou, and yet, if a child
Molest thee, pitiful and mild;
And always thy delight is, simply neat,
To seat thee faithful at thy master's feet;—

And thou, good friend and strong,
Who art the docile labourer of the world;
Who groanest when the battle mists are curled
On the red plain; who toilest all day long

To make our gain or sport; who art the care
That cleanses idle lives, which, but for thee
And thy pure, noble nature, perhaps might sink
To lower levels, born of lust and drink,
And half-forgotten sloughs of infamy,
Which desperate souls could dare;—
And ye, fair timid things, who lightly play
By summer woodlands at the close of day;—
What are ye all, dear creatures, tame or wild?
What other nature yours than of a child,
Whose dumbness finds a voice mighty to call,
In wordless pity, to the souls of all
Whose lives I turn to profit, and whose mute
And constant friendship links the man and brute?
Shall I consent to raise
A torturing hand against your few and evil days?

Shall I indeed delight
To take you helpless kinsmen, fast and bound,
And while ye lick my hand
Lay bare your veins and nerves in one red wound,
Divide the sentient brain;
And while the raw flesh quivers with the pain,
A calm observer stand,

To the Tormentors.

And drop in some keen acid, and watch it bite
The writhing life : wrench the still beating heart,
And with calm voice meanwhile discourse, and bland.
To boys who jeer or sicken as they gaze,
Of the great Goddess Science and her gracious ways ?

Great Heaven! this shall not be, this present hell,
And none denounce it; well I know, too well,
That Nature works by ruin and by wrong,
Taking no care for any but the strong,
Taking no care. But we are more than she ;
We touch to higher levels, a higher love
Doth through our being move.
Though we know all our benefits bought by blood,
And that by suffering only reach we good ;
Yet not with mocking laughter, nor in play,
Shall we give death or carve a life away.

And if it be indeed
For some vast gain of knowledge, I might give
These humble lives that live,
And for the race should bid the victim bleed,
Only for some great gain,
Some counterpoise of pain ;

And that with solemn soul and grave,
Like him who from the fire 'scapes, or the flood,
Who would save all, ay, with his heart's best blood,
But of his children chooses which to save!

Surely a man should scorn
To owe his weal to others' death and pain?
Sure 'twere no real gain
To batten on lives so weak and so forlorn?
Nor were it right indeed
To do for others what for self were wrong.
'Tis but the same dead creed,
Preaching the naked triumph of the strong;
And for this Goddess Science, hard and stern,
We shall not let her priests torment and burn:
We fought the priests before, and not in vain;
And as we fought before, so will we fight again.

CHILDREN OF THE STREET.

BRIGHT boys vociferous,
Girl children clamorous,
Shrill trebles echoing,
Down the long street.
Every day come they there,
Afternoon foul or fair,
Shouting and volleying.
Through wintry winds and cold,
Through summer eves of gold,
Running and clamouring.
Never a day but brings,
Ragged and thinly clad,
Waking the city air,
Battling with poverty,
Hunger, and wretchedness,
Brave little souls forlorn,
Gaining hard bread.

"Terrible accident;
Frightful explosion, Sir;
News from Australia,
News from America;
Only one halfpenny,
Special edition, Sir,
Echo, Sir, *Echo!*"

Thus they shout breathlessly,
Dashing and hurrying,
Threading the carriages,
Under the rapid feet;
Frighting the passer-by,
Down the long street:
On till they chance to meet
Some vague philosopher.

*　　　*　　　*

And straightway the hurry,
And bustle, and noise,
Fade away in his thought
Before tranquiller joys.
Here are problems indeed,
Not to solve, it is true,

But on every side filling
The fanciful view;
Which ere he has grasped them
Are vanished and gone,
But leave him in solitude
Never alone.
Thoughts of Fate, and of Life,
And the end of it all,
Of the struggle and strife
Where few rise, many fall;
Thoughts of Country and Empire,
Of Future and Past,
And the centuries gliding
So slow, yet so fast.
Old fancies, yet strange,
Thoughts sad and yet sweet,
Of lives come to harvest,
And lives incomplete;
Of the slow-footed march,
Of the Infinite plan,
Bringing slowly, yet surely,
The glory of man;
Of our failures and losses,
Our victory and gain;

Of our treasure of hope
And our Present of pain.
And, higher than all,
That these young voices teach
A glowing conviction
Too precious for speech;
That somewhere down deep
In each natural soul
Sacred verities sleep,
Holy waterfloods roll;
That to young lives untaught,
Without friend, without home,
Some gleams of a light
That is heavenlier come;
That to toil which is honest
A voice calls them still,
Which is more than the tempter's
And stronger than ill.

For, poor souls, 'twere better,
If pleasure were all,
Not to strive thus and labour,
But let themselves fall.
They might gain, for a time,

Children of the Street.

Higher wages than this,
And that sharp zest of sinning
The innocent miss.
They might know fuller life,
And, should fortune befriend,
Escape the Law's pains
From beginning to end.
Or, if they should fail,
What for them does home bring
Which should make of a prison
So dreadful a thing?
These children, whom formalists,
Narrow and stern,
Have denied what high principle
Comes from to learn;
To whom this great empire,
Whose records they cry,
Is a book sealed as close
As the ages gone by;
Who bear a name great
Among nations of earth,
But are English alone
By the fortune of birth;
These young mouths that come

To a board well-nigh bare,
Who elsewhere were riches,
But here a grave care.

Great Empire! fast bound
By invisible bands,
That convey to earth's limits
Thy rulers' commands;
Who sittest alone
By thy rude northern sea,
On an ocean-built throne,
The first home of the free,
Whom thy tall chimneys shroud
In a life-giving gloom;
Who clothest mankind
With the work of thy loom;
Who o'er all seas dost send out
Thy deep-laden ships;
Who teachest all nations
The words of thy lips;
Who dispatchest thy viceroys
Imperially forth
To the palms of thy East
And the snows of thy North;

Who holdest vast empires
Of dark subtle men
By the might of just laws
And the sword of the pen;
Who art planted wherever
A white foot may tread,
On the poisonous land
Which for ages lies dead;
Who didst nourish the freeman
With milk from thy breast,
To the measureless Commonwealth
Lording the West;
Who holdest to-day
Of those once subject lands
A remnant too mighty
For weaklier hands;
Who in thy isle-continent,
Hourly increased,
Rearest empires of freemen
To sway the far East;
Who art set on lone islets
Of palm and of spice,
On deserts of sand
And on mountains of ice;

Who bring'st Freedom wherever
Thy flag is unfurled :
The exemplar, the envy,
The crown of the World !

What is't thou dost owe
To these young lives of thine,
What else but to foster
This dim spark divine ?
Think of myriads like these
Without teaching or home,
Who with pitiful accents
Beseeching thee come ;
Think how Time, whirling on,
Time that never may rest,
Brings the strength of the loins
And the curve of the breast,
Till, with poor minds still childish,
These children are grown
To the age that shall give them
Young lives of their own ;
Think of those, who to-day
In the sweet country air
Live, as soulless, almost,

As the birds which they scare;
Think of all those for whom,
To the immature brain,
The dull whirr of the loom
Brings a throbbing of pain;
Think of those poor lives fallen
Which never shall rise,
For the lack of the warning
Their country denies,—
Fallen, ruined, and lost,
Through all time that shall be,
Fallen for ever and lost
To themselves and to thee;—
Thou who standest, girt round
By strong foes on each side,
Foes who envy thy greatness,
Thy glory, thy pride;
Thou, who surely shalt need
Heart and soul, brain and hand,
Brain to plan, hand to bleed,
For thy might, O dear land!

* * *

Till, while slowly he pondered
These thoughts in his brain,
See! there swiftly comes rushing
A young troop again.

" Terrible accident;
Frightful explosion, Sir;
News, Sir, from Germany;
Latest from India;
Special edition, Sir,
Only one half-penny !"
Thus the revoluble
Assonant *Echo*

Again they shout breathlessly;
Dashing and hurrying,
Frighting the passer-by,
Shouting and volleying,
Bright boys vociferous,
Girl-children clamorous,
On till they meet again
Some vague philosopher.

SONG.

AH! well knows the poet that life is brief,
Brief and fleeting, though knowledge is long.
Death a murderer, Time a thief,
And some passionate cry of a secular wrong,
And some under-wail of a half-veiled grief:
'Tis that sweetens his song.

For what, then, is life and the days that are done
But the trivial tale of each fugitive day?
'Tis but a rising and setting of sun.
And the songs are all dumb, and the birds fled away;
And the flowers as they fade, and the streams as they run,
Proclaim him as they.

Consider he must, though the sum of his thought
Were only assurance that thought is vain,
False, and fleeting, and uselessly sought;
Barren and false as the sands of the main:
A hopeless, perpetual quest, that is sought
For ever in vain.

A SEPARATION DEED.

Whereas we twain, who still are bound for life,
Who took each other for better and for worse,
Are now plunged deep in hate and bitter strife,
And all our former love is grown a curse;
So that 'twere better, doubtless, we should be
In loneliness, so that we were apart,
Nor in each other's changed eyes looking see
The cold reflection of an alien heart:
To this insensate parchment we reveal
Our joint despair, and seal it with our seal.

Forgetting the dear days not long ago,
When we walked slow by starlight through the corn;
Forgetting, since our hard fate wills it so,
All but our parted lives and souls forlorn;
Forgetting the sweet fetters strong to bind
Which childish fingers forge and baby smiles,
Our common pride to watch the growing mind,
Our common joy in childhood's simple wiles,
The common tears we shed, the kiss we gave,
Standing beside the open little grave;

A Separation Deed.

Forgetting these and more, if to forget
Be possible, as we would fain indeed.
And if the past be not too deeply set
In our two hearts, with roots that, touched, will bleed;
Yet, could we cheat by any pretext fair
The world, if not ourselves—'twere so far well—
We would not put our bonds from us, and bare
To careless eyes the secrets of our hell;
So this indenture witnesseth that we,
As follows here, do solemnly agree.

We will take each our own, and will abide
Separate from bed and board for all our life;
Whatever chance of weal or woe betide,
Nought shall re-knit the husband and the wife.
Though one grow gradually poor and weak,
The other, lapt in plenty, will not heed;
Though one, in mortal pain, the other seek,
The other may not answer to the need;
We, who through long years did together rest
In wedlock, heart to heart, and breast to breast.

One shall the daughter take, and one the boy,—
Poor boy, who shall not hear his mother's name,

K

Nor feel her kiss; poor girl, for whom the joy
Of her sire's smile is changed for sullen shame :
Brother and sister, who, if they should meet,
With faces strange, amid the careless crowd,
Will feel their hearts beat with no quicker beat,
Nor inward voice of kinship calling loud :
Two widowed lives, whose fulness may not come ;
Two orphan lives, knowing but half of home.

We have not told the tale, nor will, indeed,
Of dissonance, whether cruel wrong or crime,
Or sum of petty injuries which breed
The hate of hell when multiplied by time,
Dishonour, falsehood, jealous fancies, blows,
Which in one moment wedded souls can sunder ;
But, since our yoke intolerable grows,
Therefore we set our seals and souls as under :
Witness the powers of wrong and hate and death,
And this indenture also witnesseth.

AN ODE TO FREE ROME.

LEAP, all ye seven hills; be glad, O hallowed ground,
Built up of ruin through the infinite years;
Be glad, and let the sound
Of joy arise, of joy unmixed with tears,
Till all the sacred dust beneath
Quicken from out the grasp of death,
And Kingdom, Commonwealth, and Empire each,
The will to govern and the brain to teach,
Warrior and jurist, and the eloquent tongue,
The plastic hand of art, the holy fire of song,
Live once again, if ever they were dead.
For now the night is past, the dawn is come;
The strength of evil spent, the black dream fled,
After the age-long gloom the heavens grow red.
Man, exiled long, turns to his ancient home:
Once more, with longing hearts, the nations yearn;
Once more they call, with lips and eyes that burn,
Thy name, regenerate Rome!

Old art thou, Rome, and worn :
So old that scarce our eyes can trace
The sum of centuries on thy face.
So thick beneath thy soil the empires lie
That Heaven's own air above thee seems to die;
And on thy plains forlorn
By night the plague-mist broods with ghastly breath,
And the chill leprous vapours settle down
Even to the shrunken limits of the town.
Old art thou, and to-day thy Romans dwell
Nestling within the broken shell
Of palace and of temple, and the hand
Of cunning, vanished skill shines through the wall
Of humble hovels tottering to their fall;
And oft the delvers 'mid thy ruins start
To see some breathing miracle of art;
And fair tall columns stand,
Amid the sordid present, like the ghost;
Showing from out the meanness of to-day
The high hope sunk, the ruin, the decay,
Of some once great ideal spent and lost.

Thou wert not pure nor good,
O Rome, in those great days our hearts recall.

On violence thy growing power was built,
On violence and guilt;
The simpler lives that made thy Commonwealth,
The general sober health,
Were lived for power, and that through weary time
The triumph to the Capitol might climb,
With Death in its train; and long before thy fall
Thy sated eyes were daily drunk with blood,
Thy pitiless hands were busy with scourge and chain.
A proud cold mistress wert thou, stern and grave,
Trampling out life and freedom from thy slave,
Till the rude wild barbarians, one by one,
Lost the fair pride and vigour of the free,
And for their gods took luxury and thee.
And ere thy race was run
Thy mailëd legions, speeding fast and far,
O'er land and sea had borne the blight of war,
Till the world lay asleep,
And one foul canker of ignoble peace
Consumed thee, slow and deep;
And amid dreamy languors of delight,
And hot red flushes mixt of lust and blood,
Rose-crowned thou satest, thy weary eyes aglow
With death-throes of the nude young limbs below;

And fierce prætorians hurling down
The hardly conquered blood-stained crown;
And poison and plot, and nameless sloughs of sin.
These were the joys thou gavest thy soul to win;
These the dead centuries brought, nor seemed as they
    would cease.

And then thou wert divided, and the rude
Fierce savage from the boundless plain laid bare
Thy fertile fields, and the slow-stealing tide
Of ruin, oft beat back, broke high and higher,
And low and lower; like a dying fire
Thy empire sank, till sink it might no more.
And after long, long years
Of rapine and of tears,
Thou, the corrupt, the lewd,
Forgetting all thy life that was before,
The guilty, gave thy harlot limbs to wear
The white robes of the saintly crucified;
And with vain sacrifice and heathen rite,
And re-established idols, and the steam
Of thy discarded censers, thou didst turn
The God-sent words that burn,
The pure commands of light,

Into a sickly sensual dream;
And over all the past
Didst such strange glamour cast,
That thou, who once wert drunk with blood of saint
And martyr—thou, who once didst flout and scorn
The grand old kingdoms not of thee,
Didst stoop to bend a lowly knee
To a poor fisher, Hebrew born.
Him by a foolish fable didst thou take
For priest and ruler; and, with craft to make
All things thy own, once more thou didst regain
Thy old bad rule; and threats of pain
And promise; bound with fierce constraint
Thy conquerors, till thou cam'st to be
The mistress of the world, the foe of all the free.

And then, oh Rome,
Began thy worst abasement; for till now
Thy vices were the vices of the strong,—
Thy life as theirs in whom the tide
Runs over-strong, and the hot pride
Of life and all its fires so fiercely glow,
That scarce amid the tumult and the throng
They hear the sweet old voices come,

Telling of innocence and home.
For always 'mid the turmoil and the din
Of passion and the long laborious sin
Pure voices rose : sweet bursts of song,
Sage words of wisdom, histories fair,
Immortal codes of laws, which still
Downward the grateful centuries bear,
Rhetoric which shall scarcely die,
Philosophies remote and high,
And breathing art ; and through the long
Ages, one firm unswerving will
Moulding the world, till man became
Roman in soul and name.

But now thou knew'st to take
Another form of rule, and thou, who erst
Didst march with mail-clad warriors, battling down
Opposing wills, and first among the first,
Won'st from a conquered world the hard-earned crown,
Now like a cold black snake
Around the blighted souls of men didst glide,
And with feigned messages of doom,
And monstrous fable and immoral threat,
A womanish, subtle conqueror, didst set

Thy foot upon mankind; nor trick, nor cheat,
Nor secret craft, nor wile, nor dark deceit,
Nor hypocrite pretence didst leave untried,
Nor thought nor deed of gloom.
Thy empire thou didst base on groans and sighs
Of lifelong captives shut from life and love,
And at thy bidding all the sacred ties
Of home thou didst unloosen and remove—
All thought but thought for thee. So didst thou build
Thy throne on suffering; while thy pontiffs sate
'Mid well-carved nymphs and pictures fair,
And pagan joyance everywhere,
And made their atheist fancies bold
With philosophic sneers of old,
As the augurs did; and in the sacred name
Of God, careless, and flushed with wine, they filled
The sanctuary with revel, and the shame
Of lust of power and greed insatiate;
And scoffed at Christ, and mocked the zeal
Of those too faithful souls and pure,
Whom faster far than chains of steel
Their high religion could immure,
And who, from convent prisons sad,
Their impious feasts made glad.

Or these lewd triflers passed; and then,
Worse tyranny of purer men,
Stern zealots who, believing, sought
To kill the sacred life of thought
By scourge, and chain, and axe, and stake,
And o'er mind's seething ocean spread
Such calm as when the winds are dead;
And not in vain, for year by year,
Brought low by horrid chills of fear,
The world's high pulse beat weak and faint,
Till lying vision of sickly saint
And fabulous dogma could replace
The Pagan tenderness and grace.
And o'er all lands thy priests swarmed far and near,
Close to the blood-stained rulers' dying ear,
With venal gloss for unrepented sin,
And secret absolution, and did win
The credulous faith of woman; and if e'er
Some bolder soul, grown jealous, turned to God
From all thy forgeries, it with dreadful fear,
And chain, and dungeon, and the iron rod,
And blood and fire, thou didst subdue
To thine own ends, and with a hideous skill
Thou madest the whole world bow before thy will,

Till thy vast fable grew
To a black nightmare, blighting heart and soul;
And ever with thy prisons filled with pain,
And thy dark shadow, blasting the world's brain.
So long time did the weary centuries roll,
And thou didst wax and batten on the blood
Of the innocent and good.

And then there came
Another dawn with thunders, and the flame
Of its red lightning flashed from soul to soul,
And thought a waking giant rose and broke
Thy hateful bonds, and soared to heaven and spoke
The godlike words which erst thou didst control.
And the dread salutary storm of war
Burst o'er unhappy Europe far;
And the brave North from out its cold
Gray, frozen plains rushed forth to meet
The Pagan South, which at thy feet
Had spent its manhood : and the bold
High soul of England, she who sate
Behind her sea-cliffs isolate.
These spurned thy hateful yoke and thee,
And, taking heart, grew great and free,

And overspread the world; but thou,
Knowing the voice of doom,
Ruthless, with fire and sword didst trample out
The nascent soul within thee, and enslave
The whole fair South in blackest depths of gloom.
There, in an ignorance too dark for doubt,
And a worse death than that which feeds the grave,
Thou didst engulf her. There did she remain,
Dead, while life surged around her; joy, and pain,
High hopes, and aspirations, all forgot.
There, chained to earth, the nations grovelled and were
    not,
And there some grovel now.

Ah! glorious city, what pangs were thine
In those long shameful years!
Cold as a corpse round which the graveclothes twine,
Thou drank'st the cup of tears;
Thy vesture they divided, and did tear
In sunder thy own Italy, fair and sweet.
And thou could'st bear
To see her trampled under alien feet!
Sometimes thy sons, filled with such holy fire
As in all time doth patriot hearts inspire,

Would rear thy fallen Commonwealth once more
In vain, or else by burning words would strive
To make the dry bones of thy Empire live;
And then time fled, and voice and arm would fail,
And death and silence reign. The day of doom,
Which touched the souls of men with tongues of flame,
Broke not on thee. Upon thy living tomb
Of that great travail whence the freeman came,
Stole but a passing murmur, quickly gone;
And then thy hateful life crept smoothly on,
Untroubled, as before. The tyrants slew
And worked their selfish schemes of petty wrong
Upon thy Italy, yet no lightning flash
Shot from thy eyes, O mighty mother, to dash
The spoiler to the earth; for thou wast bound
In womanish fetters: sunk so sad, so deep,
In such a lifeless lethargy profound,
That no cry came to break thy shameful sleep:
So well thy crafty guardians knew
To stop thy ears; while to the far
Dim ends of earth they stretched their hands,
Armed with all pitiless commands,
And mental tortures worse than death,

And sad confessions wrung from failing breath,
And stamped out thought, and strove to still
The world's great tumult to their will,
And in this shameful mould recast
Thy illimitable Past.

Slow is God's purpose deep,
And slow the cycles creep
To the full end; and we who know
Fruitless the long years come and go,
Fruitless the brief lives lived and spent
To change the old wrong impotent;
Who, while we hopeless droop and fade
Beneath thick Error's poison shade,
See it to glorious stature rise,
And lose its summit in the skies—
See a false halo shed round crime,
And error consecrate by time
Grow weary of delay, and fain
The eternal purpose to arraign.
Ah! blind and weak of faith; for, see,
When least we think the thing shall be,
By secret ways remote and still
Fares on the one unchanging will,

By trackless paths; in seasons known
By one Intelligence alone;
And oft, when least we heed or think,
Our footsteps tremble on the brink;
And often, when we seem to hold
The future, with its store of gold,
Lo! quick the fairy gleam is gone,
And leaves us hopeless and alone.

And so with thee:
The furious storm of change had passed once more
And left thee as before.
There seemed no shadow on the glaring sky,
No little cloud which any might descry;
A time no more of wild imaginings;
A time of mistresses and kings,
Secret police, confessors, Bourbons, spies,
Dark prisons filled with patriot sighs:
Rome basking, with her vulture wings outspread,
As if all nobler thoughts and dreams were dead;
O'er all our Europe not a breath or stir
But foul intrigue of king and minister,—
One deep corruption to replace
The kindly ties of common race.

Secure thou seem'dst of ruin, ay, secure;
But, God be praised, not sure.

For lo! from out that calm and silence deep,
A loud and bitter cry!
Europe, awaking from her nightmare sleep,
Lifted her voice on high;
And the peoples who long time had crouched before
That subtle deadly yoke,
Had risen again, had risen and once more
The voice of freedom spoke,—
Whispered first with a low unmeaning murmur;
Then, 'mid fire and cannon smoke,
Spoke out loud, as, with hand and voice grown firmer,
The Revolution woke.
And over many a fair and stately city
The fiend of civil strife,
Drunk with conquest, blind to reverence, dead to pity,
Rose to an awful life,—
Rose till all our Europe, trodden under
The thing the priests had wrought,
Rang with confused unmeaning thunder
Of inarticulate thought;
And the lonely dreamer, stern and crimson-handed,

And the patriot mad with hope,
And the zealot and the socialist, commanded
More than Emperor or Pope.
And they seized thee, and with joy and exultation
Baptized thee, Commonwealth;
While thy Pontiff, long perplexed 'twixt Church and nation,
Slunk out of thee by stealth.
Till the legions of thy sister, France the glorious—
She who once awoke the world—
Over liberty and commonwealth victorious,
Against thy life were hurled;
And thou sankest down at last, though battling bravely
For the freedom thou hadst won:
Never losing heart, but striving sternly, gravely,
Till hope and life were done.
And o'er every race, from Germany enlightened
To God-forgotten Spain,
The chains of the oppressor's hand were tightened,
The fetters forged again.
Once more the informer ruled, the sleek confessor
Sate by the ear of kings;
A nightmare on the race, a dark assessor
Prompting to shameful things.

"All things are mine," the priest said; "I am master
Of pomps, and thrones, and powers:"
Nor marked the shadows ever gliding faster
Of the inexorable hours!

For slowly in Time's hidden womb
Fate's secret forces did mature.
The silent energies obscure
The destinies of doom;
And tiny Piedmont, set beneath the mountain,
To one foreseeing brain
Seemed the prime source, the fair upspringing fountain
Of Italy again.
And craft, than priestcraft subtler still,
And cunning and unswerving will,
These worked in silence long; and then
The rash Triumvir, king of men,
The Roman without stain or guile,
Rushed from his rocky sea-girt isle.
And thy frank monarch marched, and he
Who France enslaved but made thee free,
And chased the spoiler out and broke his power,
And drove him, beaten back, to fort and tower:
And thou, rich Lombardy, wert free.

And over thee, fair Tuscany,
The onward flowing tide of freedom broke,
And kingdom after kingdom woke,
Till last on thee, O sweet South, bound
In utter darkness, prisoned and confined,
There broke with high tumultuous sound
An echo of the mighty northern wind.
Again the red-clad dreamer rose
And rushed unarmed upon his foes,
And did prevail—such strength there is in faith—
And did prevail.
And all the dark and hateful things that be,
All tools and instruments of tyranny,
Fell from thy limbs and left thee free ;
And at thy prison gate
And hideous, rayless cell,
No more the gaoler sate,
Making the Paradise God made, a hell.
And all was free through Italy, free, free,
From thy cold Alp to burning Sicily:
Free everywhere, O Rome, except for thee
And thy gray, silent Venice weeping by the sea.

And then thy force seemed spent again,

O Italy, and the slow crawling years
Deferred thy fullness, till thy growing pain
Prompted rash onsets checked in blood and tears ;
Yet, through defeat thou didst advance and gain
Thy Venice, and through defeat
And agony of Mentana didst advance
To destiny complete,
Till thy too jealous sister, France—
She who with foreign fanatic and fool
Did buoy thy oppressor's rule—
She, by strong blows from the victorious North,
Broken and crushed, and sunk in ruin, fell ;
And, with her trumpets sounding the swift knell
Of priestcraft, Italy marched forth,
And the priests' hirelings shrank and were afraid.
And strong and calm, and gloriously arrayed,
Thou sawest her conquering legions come ;
And not in battle guise, or hasty strength,
But after patient waiting, and at length,
Thy Italy came home !

And time it was indeed
She came ; ay, it was time ; for scarce had ceased
The boldest utterance that ever priest

Had launched against our race.
Ay! it was time indeed.
Scarce had the echoes died within the hall,
Where the weird power which tottered to its fall
Spake forth with voice and threat more bold
Than ever furious Pontiff launched of old,—
Spake forth amid the sycophant crowd,
The Jesuit suborned from every clime,
The stolid Eastern left behind of time,
The supple Italian mad for place;
And those, the shame of every freer race,
Who come to hate the liberty they know,
And thoughts and lives that grow;
Who into freemen's gatherings slip—
Smooth actors false, who play their part
With tolerance upon the lip
And tyranny at heart;
The pale apostate, worldly wise;
The trickster bland with wolfish eyes.
All these, and more, were there;
And with intrigue, and trick, and wile,
Did each indignant soul beguile,
Till the mild zealot of the pagan chair
Stood forth amid the thunder and the flame;

Stood forth—oh, blasphemy and shame!—
Infallible—oh, mighty mocking name!—
Infallible o'er peoples and o'er kings,
Infallible o'er earthly thoughts and things.
Too late to stay the madness and the crime,
Thou camest, O Italy. Ay, 'twas time, 'twas time!

Yes! it was time.
And now a Rome regenerate once more
Amid her queenly cities sits sublime.
Fair Venice, fresh like Cypris from the seas;
Ravenna, dim with hoary memories;
Milan, with spires of marble clustering white;
Genoa, on terraced hill-sides clear and bright;
Florence, the flower of cities; and thou, fair town,
On the blue crescent of whose bay,
Though dynasties and nations pass away,
The burning hill looks down
That whelmed thy sisters;—these
And others, twinkling, like the Pleiades
'Mid the large stars, with gems of form and hue
Fairer than e'er thy ancient Romans knew,
Kneel round thee where thou sittest as a Queen,
Re-clothed with all the glories that have been.

An Ode to Free Rome.

The glories? Yes, but not the might.
That to the colder North has flown,
To where she lieth—she,
The little Island under grayer light,
'Mid loud perpetual surges of the sea,
By boisterous winds o'erblown,
Seated upon two hemispheres, and can teach,
As thou couldst once, a universal speech;
Or to the vast and thinly-peopled West,
Unknown to thee, where humble homes are blest
With deep content and plenty, though the State
Grow rotten; or, it may be, to the great
Vast form which broods o'er Europe like a cloud,
As did thy Goths; or, maybe, to the strong,
Stern race of banded freemen, which grows free
Through bonds, and, gaining freedom, set thee free:
Heirs of thy mail-clad legions gone before.
Ah! mockery, that Time can do no more!

Ay! the long centuries mock us as they roll;
And we, we cannot tell
To what far goal fares on the world's great soul,
Whether to ill or well.
Art thou indeed, black ghost,

For ever taken from our eyes and fled,
Among the hateful growths long lapsed and lost,
Which now are sunk and dead?
Or shalt thou from the coward fears of men
Who hear the Atheist bray,
And morbid doubters doubting heaven away,
Grow strong to blight again?
Or shall a happier fate, great Church of old,
The hidden riches of thy life unfold—
Great Church which men have strangled!—till we see
What sacred treasures, richer far than gold,
What power of faith and ordered liberty,
Thy nursing arms enfold?
Grant it, O saints on earth and saints above,
Who have made pure her foulness with your love;
Grant it, pale monks, who from dim convent room
Saw angels through the gloom;—
Grant it, sweet ministering women; all
Who raised, who raise to-day, the feet that fall;
Who for fair works of mercy live,
To pray, to work, to succour, and to give;—
And ye who saw and drew the mother mild
Adore the Eternal Child,
Grant it, if e'er to mortal prayer 'tis given

To speed the will of Heaven;—
Grant that from out all changes there may come
A new, regenerate Rome!

We know not, but 'tis clear
Her old dominion comes not, and 'tis well;
For maybe, in some happy future near,
Or maybe distant, comes a newer birth,
A peaceful federation of the earth :
Who shall discern or tell ?
Is it a dream ? But in thy Senate, Rome,
Which was a dream, a dreamer sits to-day—
Two there were once, but one has passed away;
The mightier, amid the happy dead
He dreams not any more—
And one there is who bends a whitened head,
A happy dreamer, who fulfilled his dream,
And has attained his home,
And dreams to-day of Tiber's deepened stream
White with the sails of yore ;
And dreams along thy poisoned, lonely plain—
The work of long neglect and of the priest—
The sounds of happy toil which long have ceased,
The vine and corn again ;

The peace, the plenty, which thy Romans knew;
The glory, not the dominance of old;
The waving wheat, or maize with sheen of gold;
And, where the robber lurks upon the hill,
Again the purple clusters fill;
Science to knit a long-dissevered race,
And mild-eyed, gradual knowledge to efface,
By tranquil method subtly strong,
The centuries of ignorance and wrong;
The priest no ruler, but a friend
To guide the feeble feet that heavenward tend;
Leaving, in place of his old rule,
The simple teaching of the school,
The vespers in the twilights dim,
The children's voices in the innocent hymn,
The blessed, saintly souls which take
A life of pity for their Master's sake,
A fuller life than that the Pagan knew;
O dreamer, dream thy dream, and dream it true!

THE WRECK.

The mighty wind sings,
The maddened surge rings,
As the storm hurries by
On invisible wings;
And the sails are close furled,
And the sea-birds are whirled
Through the night with a cry;

And the great waves race past,
And the ship drives on fast
To the black rocks that frown;
And the horrible blast
With its pitiless breath,
Bringing horror and death,
Drives them on, whelms them down.

Burst and break, wind and wave!
Though no mortal may save
The dear lives you destroy,
From the depths of the grave
They shall rise, ye shall fall.
This life is not all;
Oh, great wonder and joy!

WASTED.

Sunk deep in indolent ease and sleep,
    Careless ofttimes of speech and deed,
With one ingrained conviction deep
    Of nothingness for faith and creed;

And when pain came to him, or grief,
    Leaving the world and friends behind,
And, faithful to his unbelief,
    Sowing his soul upon the wind.

And yet we loved him, and lament
    A friend unselfish, kindly, true;
A candid nature sweet, content
    To think all good of those he knew.

Without one jealous thought or low,
    Without a faith, yet faithful found;
A surface-sceptic, deep below,
    By sacred faiths obliged and bound.

Not reverent, yet holding sure
    Some secret spring of reverence;
Not innocent, yet white and pure
    In love and awe of innocence.

It must be it is well with him
    Who loved so much. Beyond our ken
He holds him, in some Eden dim,
    Who raised and blessed the Magdalen.

———o———

SURSUM!

From kingly palaces
And golden throne,
From castled battlements
Princely and lone,
From lowly cottages,
From crowded factories,
From prison-fortresses,
Awake! arise!
Awake, O souls! arise! clothe yourselves—faster, faster:
For, hark! the throng, the pomp, the trumpets of the Master.

        Ye shall not hesitate,
        Nor stay to say
        Why go we to the gate
        Ere yet 'tis day;
        Above the cataract,
        Beyond the avalanche,
        On topmost pinnacle,
        'Tis day! 'tis day!
'Tis day, O souls, 'tis day! oh, hasten—faster, faster!
How shall you naked face the eye, the gaze, of the Master?

SONG.

They mount from glory to glory,
   They sink from deep unto deep,
They proclaim their sweet passionate story,
   They tremble on chords that weep,
And with them my soul spreads her wings,
And my heart goes out to them and sings.

And chord into chord interlaces,
   Like the leaves that protect some fair bloom;
And with subtle and tremulous graces,
   And tender lights dappled with gloom,
Like the fall of an ocean-borne bell,
The harmonies quicken and swell.

Then swift from those languishing voices
   And accents which marry and die,
Like the sound of a trumpet, rejoices
   One clear note unfaltering high;
And my soul, through its magical power,
Bursts and dies like an aloe in flower.

ANCHORED.

Beyond the scorching plain
   Of the trackless rippled shore,
The heaped-up tides complain
   As if they came no more;
And in the glaring light
   Of the slow-declining day,
The far-off sails gleam white
   As the great ships go their way;
And in the cliff garden so fair
A young maid with a rose in her hair.

The garden beds are sweet
   With their shining laurel bowers,
Soft turf for lightsome feet,
   Heart's-ease and gilly-flowers,
Lush roses white and red,
   And speckled lilies large,
Passion-flowers overhead,
   Framing the blue sea-marge;
But from the sweet blooms at her side
Her eyes look out over the tide.

And suddenly there springs
  Upon the wide sea plain,
A breeze like fanning wings,
  And life revives again.
The pearly lines of foam
  Steal onwards, crisp and sweet,
Till to the cliffs they come,
  And eddy at their feet ;
And wavelet on wavelet the tide
Races on through the harbour wide.

And the stranded hulls which lay
  All the long day black and dead,
Swing round to the freshening spray,
  And spread their white wings overhead ;
And the gulls mew their strange sea song,
  And all sea things that be,
On the hot sand fainting long,
  Revive with the kiss of the sea ;
And a sail comes up, ghostly and white,
To where it shall sojourn to-night.

And over the harbour bar,
  Within the deep-sunk pier,

While the sunset glows afar,
   The homeward ship draws near;
And, lo! one with straining sight
   Upon the broad deck sees
A waving gleam of white
   Up amid the garden trees;
And the anchor leaps out with deep sound,
And two hearts with it bound after bound.

And when twilight begins to fade,
   Just before the low-hung moon,
Through the perfumed garden shade
   The full waves murmur a tune.
Heart's-ease and gilly-flowers,
   Lush roses white and red,
And amid the happy bowers
   The passion-flowers overhead:
Ah, Time, that thy steps are so fleet!
Ah, Life, thou art fair! thou art sweet!

SOULS IN PRISON.

I THOUGHT that I looked on the land of the lost,
A stony desert, arid and bare,
Gray under a heavy air.

Not a bird was there, nor a flower, nor a tree,
Nor rushing river, nor sounding sea;
And I seemed to myself like a ghost.

A land of shadows, a herbless plain,
A faint light aslant on the barren ground,
And never a sight nor a sound:

Only at times, of invisible feet,
Wearily tracking one dull, sad beat,
Too spiritless to complain;

And of faces hid by a blank white mask,
From which there glared out cavernous eyes,
Full of hate and revolt and lies :

As if the green earth on which others live
Had nothing of hope or of fear to give
But a hopeless, perpetual task.

Far in the distance a vast grey pile
Stretched out its spider-like, echoing ways
In long centrifugal rays ;

And sometimes dimly I seemed to see
Dumb gangs of poor workers, fruitlessly
Bent in hard tasks useless and vile,

To which, issuing silent, in single rank,
Along narrow pathways stony and blank
The hopeless toilers would come.

Or else each was idly cooped in a cell
Narrow, and gloomy, and hard, as hell,
Which was all that they knew of home.

And around them frowning, grimy and tall,
With no ivy or lichen, a circling wall
Shut God and life utterly out;

And in the midst, with unclosing eye,
A muffled watcher stood silently,
As they paced about and about.

Never alone—for, wherever they went,
From some central tower an eye was bent
Along all the long, straight-drawn ways.

Never alone—for an unseen eye,
As the stealthy footstep went noiselessly by,
Swept each lonely cell with its gaze.

Always alone—for in all the throng
No word or glance as they shuffled along
But the order-word, sharp and loud.

Always alone—for in all the crowd
No glance of comfort from pitying eyes
Might pierce through the thick disguise.

Nor, if husband were there, or child, or wife,
Could the subtle communion of love and life
Escape that terrible eye.

Yet husbands and wives and children there were,
Young limbs, and age bent in a dumb despair,
Too strong or too weak to die.

Nothing remained, as it seemed, but thought
Of the old hopes vanished and come to nought,
And the hopeless, perpetual care,—

Nought but to sit, as the night would fall,
Tracing black ghosts on the blank white wall
In a silent rage of despair;

Or, before the dull daylight began to break,
To start at the iron-tongued summons and wake
To the curse of another day.

And so, in silence, to brood and plot
To regain the poor freedom and life which were not,
Though it bartered a soul away;

Or, later, to cherish the old offence
With a secret lurking devil of sense,
And a spring of desire self-bent,

Till at last all longing was sunk and spent
In a lifeless, fathomless slough of content.
Not repentance, nor fear, nor grief,

Nor belief at all, nor yet unbelief;
But a soul which skulks from itself like a thief,
And is damned for ever and dead.

*   *   *   *   *

Thus I thought to myself; and, though straight I saw
It was only the house of retributive Law,
I shuddered and shrank, and fled.

FREDERIC.

As these sheets came in from the printer,
    My lad who had brought me them said,
"Please, Sir, as I passed his office,
    They told me that Frederic was dead."

And I knew in a moment thrill through me,
    First a keen little pang and smart,
Then a sudden revolt and rebellion
    Seize on me and fill my heart,

As he went on with boyish prattle,
    Before I had courage to speak :
"He died of consumption, they said, Sir ;
    And he earned sixteen shillings a week."

"How old was he?" "Just seventeen, Sir:
    He had grown very tall and white."
And I thought of the childish features,
    The bright cheeks, and the eyes still more bright,

When, withdrawn from his school far too early,
    He came with his treasured prize,
To show to his new-found master,
    With a simple pride in his eyes;

And how it soon proved that his writing
    Was so clear, and skilful, and fine,
That I set him the task to decipher
    The hieroglyphs which are mine.

'Twas four years ago; and so splendid
    Did my first book of songs appear,
That, though ofttimes already rejected,
    I despatched them this time without fear.

Nor in vain. And now many friends know them,
    And critics are kindly in praise,
But the cold little hand that adorned them
    Has cast up the brief sum of its days.

Sixteen shillings! this pittance could purchase
    The flower of those boyish years!
This could narrow that humble ambition
    To dull entries, whose total is tears!

This young life which was bursting to blossom,
  Which had borne its own fruitage one day,
Had those budding days mingled together
  Slow labour with healthfuller play.

Is it man that has done this, or rather,
  These dead blasts that blow, blow, blow, blow,
Week by week, month by month, till beneath them
  Life withers and pulses beat slow?

The dull winds that to-day are slaying
  Young and old with their poisonous breath,
Which slew the rash singer who praised them,
  Not the less with a premature death.

Is it man with bad laws and fools' customs,
  False pride, poverty, ignorant greed?
Is it God making lives for His pleasure,
  Dooms these innocent victims to bleed?

Great riddle which one day shall be clearer,
  Be our doubts with all reverence said;
But a strong power constrained me to write them,
  When I heard little Frederic was dead.

TO MY MOTHERLAND.

DEAR motherland, forgive me, if too long
I hold the halting tribute of my song;
Letting my wayward fancy idly roam
Far, far from thee, my early home.
There are some things too near,
Too infinitely dear
For speech; the old ancestral hearth,
The hills, the vales that saw our birth,
Are hallowed deep within the reverent breast:
And who of these keeps silence, he is best.

Yet would not I appear,
Who have known many a brighter land and sea
Since first my boyish footsteps went from thee,
The less to hold thee dear;
Or lose in newer beauties the immense
First love for thee, O birth-land, which fulfils

My inmost heart and soul,—
Love for thy smiling and sequestered vales,
Love for thy winding streams which sparkling roll
Through thy rich fields, dear Wales,
From long perspectives of thy folded hills.

Ay! these are sacred, all;
I cannot sing of them, too near they are.
What if from out thy dark yews, gazing far,
I sat and sang, Llangunnor! of the vale
Through which fair Towy winds her lingering fall,
Gliding by Dynevor's wood-crowned steep,
And, alternating swift with deep,
By park and tower a living thing
Of loveliness meandering;
And traced her flowing, onward still,
By Grongar dear to rhyme, or Drysllwyn's castled hill,
Till the fresh upward tides prevail,
Which stay her stream and bring the sea-borne sail,
And the broad river rolls majestic down
Beneath the gray walls of my native town.

Would not my fancy quickly stray
To thee, sea-girt St. David's, far away,

A minster on the deep; or, further still,
To you, grand mountains, which the stranger knows
Eryri throned amid the clouds and snows,
The dark lakes, the wild passes of the north;
Or Cader, a stern sentinel looking forth
Over the boisterous main; or thee, dear Isle
Not lovely, yet which canst my thought beguile—
Mona, from whose fresh wind-swept pastures came
My grandsire, bard and patriot, like in name
Whose verse his countrymen still love to sing
At bidding-feast or rustic junketing?

Ah, no! too near for song, and ye too near,
My brethren of the ancient race and tongue;
The bardic measures deep, the sweet songs sung
At congresses, which fan the sacred fire
Which did of old your ancestors inspire;
The simple worship sternly pure,
The faith unquestioning and sure,
Which doth the priest despise and his dark ways,
And riseth best to fullest praise
Beneath some humble roof-tree, rude and bare,
Or through the mountains' unpolluted air;
Who know not violence nor blood,

And who, if sometimes ye decline from good,
Sin the soft sins which gentler spirits move,
Which warmer Fancy breeds, and too much love.

I may not sing of you,
Or tell my love—others there are who will,
Who haply bear not yet a love so true
As that my soul doth fill—
If to applause it lead, or gain, or fame;
Better than this it were to know the pain
Which comes to higher spirits when they know
They fire in other souls no answering glow:
Love those who love me not again,
And leave my country nought, not even a name.

FINIS.

Caxton Printing Works, Beccles.

SONGS OF TWO WORLDS.

(SECOND SERIES.)

OPINIONS OF THE PRESS.

"Some three years ago a first batch of 'Songs of Two Worlds' called forth favourable comments from several competent critics. In some of them the rhyme was woven with art and melody, to represent the beautiful things of external life; others evinced a scholar's insight into deeper philosophies, and bespoke habitual converse with classic models. We are glad to find that there is a sufficient number of readers of healthy poetry to have encouraged this second venture.

"In earnestness, sweetness, and the gift of depicting nature, the writer may be pronounced even now a worthy disciple of his compatriot, Henry Vaughan, the silurist. . . . Several of the shorter poems are instinct with a noble purpose and a high ideal of life. One perfect picture, marginally annotated, so to speak, in the speculations which it calls forth from the writer, is 'The Organ-Boy.' But the most noteworthy poem is the 'Ode on a Fair Spring Morning,' which has somewhat of the charm and truth to nature of 'L'Allegro and Il Penseroso.' As a whole this ode is perhaps the nearest approach to a masterpiece in the volume. We can find no fault with it unless it be a seeming violation in the unities, and we cannot find too much praise for its noble assertion of man's resurrection and renovation."—*Saturday Review*, May 30th.

"In everything that respects form it would have been very difficult indeed to surpass some of the poems in the earlier series, to which we tried to do justice at the time of their appearance. If in any respect this second series can be said to be superior to the first, it is in a certain mellowness and warmth of tone of which hardly more than the promise was given in the earlier book. The very first poem in the volume is proof of this. It is styled, 'To an Unknown Poet,' and is a reminiscence of the writings of Henry Vaughan, the silurist, whose quaint, tender reveries, breathing health, as they come to us across what seems an artificial atmosphere, well deserve the celebration. It is a wonderful combination of insight, melody, picture, and suggestion, and it is as finished as it is full of subdued emotion. 'The Organ-Boy' brings out a strong contrast in a most powerful and felicitous way; the 'Ode on a Fair Spring Morning' is full of touches that show how deeply the spirit of this singer has been moved by many of the grand problems of the time, and indeed there is a whole section of the poem which might be profitably analysed on this ground had we but space."—*British Quarterly Review*, July 1st.

OPINIONS OF THE PRESS (continued).

"This volume is a real advance on its predecessor of the same name, and contains at least one poem of great originality, as well as many of much tenderness, sweetness, and beauty. The poem which marks the volume as that of a man who has a poetic initiative of his own, as well as a considerable power of expression for the commoner moods and feelings, is the very striking one on 'The Organ-Boy,' which we have read again and again, with fresh pleasure on every reading. It is to our minds a little poem of which even a first-rate poet might be proud. The very graphic picture of the little Italian boy, with which it opens, so soon passing into a reverie on the past history of the wonderful nation from which these picturesque little immigrants come to us . . . the stately passage on the destinies of England, and the graceful description of the childish crowd flocking about the Italian organ-boy and enjoying his music, at the close, make altogether as exquisite a little poem of ten pages as we have read for many a day. But we must not lead our readers to suppose that this very beautiful poem, though far the finest in the volume, is at all alone in its power to fascinate them. We earnestly hope that the third series, of which the author holds out some promise, may be as much of an advance on the second as the second is on the first, and, if so, that his poetic publications will not end there, but that he will attempt something of more solid and lasting mould."—*Spectator*, June 13th.

"Some of his smaller lyrics are very perfect, and bear the marks of careful finish and the advantage of that good taste, which is a sixth sense—essence and completion of all the rest—to writers in general. His larger poems charm us less. He has caught the true cadence from the Herricks and Lovelaces. . . . This is the very daintiest of love-making, and we do not know that any one else quite modern has done it so well. The verses—though there is a line or two which might be mended—are full of melodious charm, and sing themselves almost without music. If we have got a new maker of songs in the 'New Writer,' we may well congratulate ourselves and all the world of singers."—*Blackwood's Magazine*, August 1st.

"When two years ago the first series of 'Songs of Two Worlds' appeared, we did not join the loud chorus of praise. We could of course see in it much that was beautiful, but also much which was vague and crude. We are bound to say that the second series is a very great improvement upon the first. The writer has gained a greater mastery over the mere mechanism of verse. He has acquired, too, a vigour of style without losing any of the tenderness and mystic feeling which distinguished his earlier poems."—*Westminster Review*, July 1st.

"There are perhaps fewer marks of sustained effort in the second series of 'Songs of Two Worlds' than appeared in the earlier series which 'A New Writer' gave to the world some two years ago. But a warm welcome is due to this pleasant and able volume of poems, which is marked by distinctness of aim, artistic clearness of execution, and that particular imaginative lustre which

OPINIONS OF THE PRESS (continued).

belongs to the truly poetic mind. The author has learned in many schools without any sacrifice of his own individuality. He often recalls Wordsworth, but not a Wordsworth who, when experience had calmed the hot passions and dissipated the extravagant hopes of youth, could turn himself aside from painful problems, or look at them only when reflected on the face of nature, as on a still lake. The 'New Writer' is a man of his day, seeing beauty and yet coping with difficulties; at one time bursting into a pleasant love song, at another facing the obstinate questionings of intellect, or trying what light can be thrown by imagination into the depths of science."—*Guardian*, Sept. 16th.

"We have already had occasion so highly to commend the author of 'Songs of Two Worlds,' that praise now seems almost superfluous. But we may congratulate the anonymous author on having faithfully performed the rich promise which was held forth in his first book. It seems that the world may expect a third and final volume; none will welcome its appearance more gladly than ourselves, and no one will more sincerely regret that it should be the writer's last. When this author first challenged the public we were amongst the first to recognise the sterling merit of his verses and to predict for him a possible future; now we are naturally glad to see that he has not falsified our prediction. There is, as a rule, the same power of rhythm, the same facility of rhyme, the same deep thought underlying delicacy of diction which distinguished the earlier issue. As songs nothing could surpass some of the shorter pieces."—*Graphic*, Oct. 17th.

"This second series is in every sense a continuation of the first. It will be gratefully welcomed by all who have read the first, as a help to the more intimate knowledge of a poet whose first work came so unmistakably out of an admirable and amiable nature; but it opens up no new vein of feeling, and marks no new stage in the writer's mastery of verse. In this second series there are fewer traces than in the first of the writer's spiritual struggles in his search through sciences and creeds for a resting-place of belief; we see here rather the victory of the heart over the distresses of the intellect. We are glad that the writer promises a third series, and we hope that we shall have more in the vein of the 'Ode on a Fair Spring Morning,' and the exquisitely written ballad of 'Gilbert Beckett and the Fair Saracen.'"—*Examiner*, June 6th.

"It is sometimes easier to speak of a second book than of a first, because a critic has only to consider the quality of an author's success when the public has determined the quantity of the success already. The reception of the 'New Writer's' first series shows that, in his degree, he is one of the poetical forces of the time. . . . Of the school of poetry of which Horace is the highest master the 'New Writer' is a not undistinguished pupil. 'In Memory of a Friend' reminds us of Matthew Arnold by the union of clearness, sobriety, and refinement, though the 'New Writer,' with less elevation, less subtlety, and less austerity, has more warmth and perhaps more care."—*Academy*, August 11th.

OPINIONS OF THE PRESS (continued).

"Of the first series of 'Songs of Two Worlds' by a 'New Writer' we spoke with high praise. The author, whose name remains even now concealed and unknown, although the success of his first work is undoubted, has just issued a second—a volume, we think, far in advance of the earlier one—more mature, less imitative, and possessing in a greater degree those excellences which made the former one so remarkable. The diction is even more exquisite and polished; there is the same unmistakable lyrical cry, albeit its tone is somewhat subdued; the same broad human sympathy, the same deep reverent spirit, the same grace and purity, resembling the beauty and repose of the statue rather than the loveliness of the living form. . . . How different in execution and spirit is this exquisite song to much that is styled genuine poetry at the present day. The irreverent, the intolerant, the indelicate, should all ponder well over many pieces in this volume, they will be made stronger in faith, more charitably inclined, purer, and more manly, if they will only learn aright the lessons taught. Their love for what is beautiful in nature will be increased, and they will have a deeper sympathy with their fellow-men."—*Civil Service Gazette*, May 23rd.

"When the first series of 'Songs of Two Worlds' appeared we were glad to welcome a singer who showed such depth of insight and imagination, whose verse was marked by such simplicity and melody of expression. As is not very often the case with a second series, this one is superior to the first. It reveals not only the same chastity and clearness of form, the same depth and genuineness of experience, but here and there more warmth of colouring, and we are fain to think this book will raise the reputation of the writer and gain him a hearing where before, owing to a certain reserve and 'cultured calm,' he might have been denied it, or have been but tentatively read. Clear it is that no person of the least sensitiveness could read a few pages of this volume and deny that the writer possesses the 'vision of the poet.' The glance, the touch, the hint, the suggestion, suffices, and you have not only a picture but a series of pictures; the imagination is moved, and in being moved is satisfied. In that remarkable poem, 'The Organ-Boy,' we not only have a picture but a contrast, which reveals to us implicitly (as of course should be the case) a whole philosophy of national greatness and causes of decline. We wish we had space to quote at length from the poem with which this volume opens. 'To an Unknown Poet' (Henry Vaughan, the silurist) is very stately, sweet, and finished, and indicates to us several affinities of the author, giving it thus a determined critical value. Of the poems we can say no more and no less than this, that they are quick with wisdom and high thought, touched with phantasy, and flowing easily into imaginative forms, which calls readily to its service an exquisite sense of the music of words."—*Nonconformist*, June 24th.

SONGS OF TWO WORLDS.

(THIRD SERIES.)

OPINIONS OF THE PRESS.

"The third series is not unworthy of its predecessors. It presents the same command of metre and diction, the same contrasts of mood, the same grace and sweetness, perhaps the same strength and weakness, as the volumes which have already met with so favourable a reception. The writer has ample command of musical and vigorous diction, and of varied and skilful rhythm. . . . To take a common and familiar object and show forth its ideal side with graceful skill and delicate imagination, to see the poetry and pathos of daily life, is the special power which he possesses ; and this he enjoys to a degree which poets of greater range might envy. . . . On the whole, it cannot be denied that he has won a definite position among contemporary English poets. If we cannot as yet place him in the front rank, yet he has written enough to show that he has powers which may some day make good his claim to it."—*Times*, October 16th.

"The new series contains, besides a number of shorter pieces, three poems of an important character, 'Evensong,' 'From Hades,' and an enthusiastic ode to Free Rome. The first-named poem shows power, thought, and courage to grapple with the profoundest problems. In the ode we acknowledge worthy treatment of the subject and passionate expression of generous sympathy. Yet we incline to hope for the development of his poetic career rather in such finished and highly-wrought pictures as 'From Hades.' The poet here exhibits a congenial grace of description and a delicate touch, which only a true scholar, who also possessed an adequate sense of the requirements of English poetry,

could apply. The author might be trusted to tread classic paths of song without fear of swerving from the clear and statuesque grace of the models. . . . The songs in this volume have in general the same excellence as those in the former series. Songs and classical sketches, however, do not content a singer of our author's aspirations, and he is never more worth a hearing than when he allows us an insight into his views of what should be a poet's scope and standard. . . . It is to be hoped he is not serious in his apparent hesitation as to continuing his labours."
—*Saturday Review*, July 31st.

"This volume is more perfect in execution than either of its predecessors. . . . The pure lyrics are sweeter and richer. . . . The poem which seems to indicate most of that rich pictorial imagination, which after all must be the main strength of the poet, is 'From Hades.' The legends of Actaeon, of Orpheus, and of Endymion are told with an originality of touch that gives them new force and beauty. Nothing could be much finer in its way than the interpretation of the transformation of Actaeon after his vision of Artemis. Of the three, however, the finest on the whole is that of Eurydice's mind as she describes her own awakening in Hades to the music of her husband's lyre. . . . The whole picture is so beautiful that we must give it complete. . . . In 'The Birth of Verse' every stanza is a little poem in itself, and yet a part of a perfect whole. Criticism is a dim and groping art at best, but in the present case it is even more dull and groping than usual, if we are mistaken in supposing that the man who wrote those stanzas ought to have in him what will give him a permanent, though probably a modest, place in the line of English poets."—*Spectator*, May 22nd.

"The author's healthiness and uprightness of feeling refresh one like a cold air after a hot and sultry day. 'The Home Altar' should in future adorn every collection of English religious verse. But by far the best poems in the book are two that stand side by side, one inaptly called a 'Song,' the other 'At Last.' The former is a very fine and delicate poem. 'At Last' is more exquisite still. . . . Not hawthorn blossom, muffling the warm earth as the slow night-wind stirs it, falls more fragrantly, more softly than the exquisite cadence of these verses. . . . The farewell that he threatens cannot be permitted. Such singers are not lightly to be spared."—*Examiner*, May 8th.

OPINIONS OF THE PRESS (continued.)

"At last we have the promised third series, and we imagine that all its readers will rejoice with us. . . . If each book that he publishes is to mark as steady improvement as have his second and third, the world may surely look for something from the New Writer which shall immortalize him and remain as a treasure to literature."—*Graphic*, June 5th.

"The concluding series of this popular work is quite worthy of its predecessors, and it is pleasant to find that the author has already begun to reconsider his intention of writing, or at any rate printing no more poetry."—*Academy*, May 29th.

"This volume will not fail to maintain the writer's reputation. It lacks none of the simplicity and clearness of his former volumes, while in depth and dramatic range it shows decided advance. There are at least two poems here which will take high rank—'Children of the Street' and 'From Hades.' The latter presents a series of pictures fresh, clear, delicate, and bathed in imaginative light. We hope that the writer's farewell may not be in any sense final."—*British Quarterly Review*, July 1st.

"The high hopes we had been led to entertain are here realized. And this is saying much. We have the same simplicity of style, the graceful ease of phrase, the subtle thought kept in due check by reference to rhythmical effects. But over and above these qualities we have now a depth of tone and colouring. The writer's dramatic range has widened. . . . At one page he is celebrating the doubts bred of science, and the Pantheism which most often flows from them, and on the next the poor little 'Arabs' enlisted in the sale of the cheap newspapers have due celebration. . . . By his emotion their situation is made to intersect with the whole mystery of life, and that more successfully than was even the case with that wonderful piece in the last volume, 'The Organ-Boy,' one of the most powerful and finished poems of the kind we have read for long. 'Evensong' is set on a higher key, and traverses a lofty range of thought and sentiment. It is quite impossible to give any idea of the stateliness and reach of this poem. We despair of doing justice to this choice volume by extract. Every page would afford remark, and tempt to analysis and characterization."—*Nonconformist*, May 19th.

OPINIONS OF THE PRESS (*continued.*)

"It would be well indeed if our more successful versifiers, as a rule, fulfilled their early promise as calmly, equably, and melodiously as the author. The plain fact is that the anonymous poet claims for the third time our attention, on grounds far more valid than those of mere novelty. His range of moral sympathy is large, his intellectual view is wide enough to embrace a great variety of subjects, and his delicate sense of verbal fitness, and the nicer shades of manner leads him to remind us continually of other writers, without any sacrifice of his own independence and originality. . . . To these examples of two manners we might add specimens of at least a third and a fourth, but a sufficiently potent individuality breathes through them all. His farewell will be reciprocated with equal cordiality, and we might add to it a sincere *au revoir* if we knew either his face or his name."—*Guardian,* September 1st.

"He does not merely, like so many of his contemporaries, possess the accomplishment of verse, but has a genuine and apparently natural gift of song. He has mastered the difficult art of writing in English."—*Daily News,* June 12th.

"Gifted with real poetic insight, with an admirable power of expression, and with a deep sympathy with the nobler currents of modern thought. . . . In all we mark those excellences which have given him a special and distinguished place amongst modern English poets."—*Leeds Mercury,* July 7th.

"The third series will do more than either of those that have preceded it to place the reputation of the writer on a high pinnacle. . . . It shows, if possible, more exquisite finish. These poems are full from beginning to end of the true spirit of poetry; they are keenly perceptive, spontaneous, and possessed by the spirit of the beautiful and true. Every piece has the simple grace and beauty, the sweetness, the honesty, the earnestness, which poetry should have. . . . The verses are like the pure running stream. You may see every thought in them as clearly as the pebbles at the bottom of a crystal brook."—*Scotsman,* May 7th.

www.ingramcontent.com/pod-product-compliance
Lightning Source LLC
Chambersburg PA
CBHW020847160426

43192CB00007B/815